Mary C. Grey is Professorial Research Fellow at St Mary's University College, Twickenham, and has held professorial chairs in the universities of Wales, Southampton and Nijmegen (the Netherlands). A Roman Catholic, she writes in the area of social justice, focusing now on reconciliation in diverse contexts. She is a founding member of a new initiative at St Mary's, InSpiRe, the Centre for Initiatives in Spirituality and Reconciliation. SPCK published some of her earliest books, *Redeeming the Dream* (1989) and *The Wisdom of Fools?* (1993). Since then, other books have been published with SCM – *Sacred Longings* (2003) – and Darton, Longman & Todd: *The Outrageous Pursuit of Hope* (2001), *Pursuing the Dream* (2005), with Rabbi Dan Cohn-Sherbok, and *To Rwanda and Back: Spirituality and Reconciliation* (2007). Her work in social justice is underpinned by 22 years of involvement in a charity she helped to found, Wells for India, which tries to enable water security in desert areas in Rajasthan.

THE ADVENT
OF PEACE

A gospel journey to Christmas

Mary C. Grey

First published in Great Britain in 2010

Society for Promoting Christian Knowledge
36 Causton Street
London SW1P 4ST
www.spckpublishing.co.uk

British Library Cataloguing-in-Publication Data
A catalogue record for this book is available from the British Library

ISBN 978–0–281–06232–4

1 3 5 7 9 10 8 6 4 2

Typeset by Graphicraft Ltd, Hong Kong
Printed in Great Britain by JF Print

Produced on paper from sustainable forests

*Dedicated to Canon Naim Ateek, founder of
the Sabeel Ecumenical Liberation Theology Center,
Jerusalem; to Zoughbi Zoughbi, director of Wi'am,
Bethlehem; and to Pastor Mitri Raheb, director of
the International Center of Bethlehem*

Contents

Acknowledgements

With thanks to Dr Toine van Teeffelen, Arab Education Institute, Bethlehem, for discussions, information and assistance; and to my colleagues at InSpiRe, the Centre for Initiatives in Spirituality and Reconciliation, at St Mary's University College, Twickenham, for providing the right context.

Introduction: the Advent journey

Once more Advent stirs up long-buried hidden yearnings and long-ings: while department stores are already seducing us with irresistible bargains for goods we do not need, and never imagined that we or our children were missing, the hearts of people of faith and vision turn to deeper desires – the peace that always seems to elude us, both personally and globally. Within Christianity, Advent focuses on jour-neying, waiting and hoping: at the end of the journey this year, as always, we will retell the Christmas story of the angels who sang of peace on earth to people of goodwill (Luke 1.14). The song points to Advent's deeper hope, our real longing – that of a new creation, creation redeemed, forgiven and reconciled. *A world at peace.* Would it be possible to retell this story, to relive this journey, in such a way as to articulate these dreams of reconciled creation, so that our lives could be reshaped by them? It would need to be a retelling, enabling us to celebrate the feast differently, with the journey to peace and reconciliation at its heart. And it would mean that when the Christmas tree is cast aside, the decorations folded away for next year, this jour-ney would carry on and its real work begin.

The peace we long for is on different levels. Before even thinking about the war scenes that fester on at a global level, we all have per-sonal issues that are hard to face – perhaps wounds from broken relationships, job disappointments, struggles with poverty and disabil-ity, living with HIV & AIDS, grief at the death of a loved one or simply the diminishment that comes with ageing and illness. Perhaps life has become devoid of meaning. Many friends and neighbours are refugees; some sought asylum here – all carry haunting memories of a homeland where they could no longer dwell, due to climate disas-ters, a genocidal regime, war or grinding poverty.

To become reconciled – to feel at peace and be forgiven, to reach contentment – is an important part of any spirituality. At another level, attaining peace-of-the-heart may be blocked by disagreements and feuds that disrupt families, communities and nations, stretching across the generations. Sometimes in family feuds people lose any sense of how the dispute began. Within Christianity, many Christian groups are at loggerheads – often exacerbated by political and economic factors. Reconciliation, far from being a possibility, is sometimes not even longed for. At the most intractable level, our world is beset by bitter conflicts that include all the aforementioned factors – from tribal conflicts, caste discrimination in India, the war in Afghanistan, the continuing conflict in the Middle East and the violence that carries on in the numerous cities.

Today there is a changed scene that offers new hope: never before has reconciliation been viewed as a public discourse involving all conflictual groups. Since the Truth and Reconciliation Commission in South Africa, in which Archbishop Desmond Tutu played such a prominent role, reconciliation has come to be seen as the key symbol that sums up hopes for justice and restoration of peace, and leads to a transformed state of affairs. Irish President Mary Robinson, at the inauguration of her presidency in Dublin Castle in 1990, placed reconciliation at the heart of her leadership, invoking the symbol of the Fifth Province of Ireland:

> As everyone knows, there are only four geographical provinces on this island. The Fifth Province is not anywhere here or there . . . It is a place within each of us, that place that is open to the other, that swinging door which allows us to venture out and others to venture in . . . While Tara was the political centre of Ireland, tradition has it that this fifth province acted as a second centre, a necessary balance. If I am a symbol of anything, I would like to be a symbol of this reconciling, healing province.[1]

This use of the concept of reconciliation opens up a vision for this book – of reconciliation as the active means of attaining peace with justice, as well as the goal of a transformed state of affairs – for all parties. It resists any cheapening version of peace without justice, peace imposed by a superior power or, in personal terms, acquiescence to another's viewpoint with loss of self-esteem.

Reconciliation is both the longed-for goal and the way to it. It is the personal journey seeking forgiveness, the community journey towards justice and the political journey towards the healing of society.

In this Advent quest for peace, the Gospels will be our tools. They set the stage for us in the holy places of the Bible lands (Nazareth, Bethlehem and Jerusalem), telling the story of Jesus' earthly ministry of reconciliation. Here the first Christians followed their own quest for peace with justice, under the Roman occupation. But they are also sacred texts for us in the present, as we set out on this journey.

Our first task will be to make connections with Middle-Eastern Christians after Jesus, and also to ask what their situation is today. Highlighting the needs of Middle-Eastern Christians in their search for peace will evoke a response from all Christians, in diverse contexts. Retelling the old story will also evoke the centrality of the need for mutual forgiveness in our own lives, and will ask us to read the Gospel stories in a way that makes this central. A focus – but not an exclusive one – on the Middle East is chosen because at the moment it is the crucible where many conflicts interlink, because it involves all Christians in a responsibility for peacemaking, and because it is the cradle where Christianity itself was born.

Bridging the gap: Christians in the Bible lands then and now

What has happened since that early whirlwind spread of the gospel around the Mediterranean, in its flourishing and its conflicts, to produce its contemporary complexities? Here I try both to create a bridge across the centuries and to show how seeds of discord with deep historical roots may not yet completely close off possibilities of reconciliation today.

The context for the writing of the four Gospels – which I am assuming were written some time between 50 and 90 AD – was one of war and rebellion,[2] namely that of the Jewish people against the Roman occupation. This meant that many of the villages – scenes in the events of the ministry of Jesus – were being destroyed. How would people remember the important events that had occurred here? Memories are crucial for encouraging people to persevere in times of conflict. It must have been the need to keep these memories alive and vibrant for fledgling Christian communities, together with the need for resources for the community conflicts that had begun to spring up, that inspired the creation of the early texts. The danger of the times in which Luke and Matthew wrote – it is thought that Mark wrote before the fall of Jerusalem in 70 AD – explains the emphasis on the consolation Jesus offers the disciples when they should face persecution (Luke 21.10–19),[3] his urgent exhortation not to give up on prayer and the plea always to put the kingdom of God above all things. Read against the contemporary occupation of Palestine by the Zionist[4] government, there is a remarkable congruence between the Roman occupation of New Testament times and the present situation. (For clarity's sake, I refer throughout to Israel and Palestine in accordance with the official terminology of current International Law, except where 'Israel' is referred to in its biblical sense, both in Old and New Testaments.) As is well known, the context of persecution followed the early Christian communities throughout its spread into the Mediterranean world as far as Rome. This would come to an end with the conversion of the Emperor Constantine (312 AD) and his imposition of the Pax Romana on the known Western world, with the consequence that Christianity became the established religion of his vast empire.

But it was not only external political regimes that caused problems for the growth of the Christian Churches. Following the missionary journeys of Paul, the Church had begun to put down roots in many countries, among different races and cultures. But as Canon Naim Ateek (founder of Sabeel[5] in Jerusalem), relates: 'Difficulties and misunderstandings began to emerge as a result of theological, political, cultural and geographical difficulties.'[6]

The Churches began to be caught up with theological controversies, mostly concerning the nature of the relationship between Jesus and God, resulting in the early Councils of Nicaea (325), Constantinople (381), Ephesus (431) and Chalcedon (451). Eventually major schisms and separations resulted into the development of the Assyrian Church of Iraq, the Coptic Church of Egypt, the Church of Ethiopia, the Syrian Orthodox and the Armenian Orthodox Churches.[7] Yet this diversity, which could have been such a source of richness, culminated in the tragic schism between Eastern and Western Churches in 1054. Today, in Jerusalem, there are thirteen separate Christian communities: six Catholic, five Orthodox, two Protestant (Anglican and

Lutheran) Churches. The next decisive event that Christianity would
encounter came in the seventh century with the rise of Islam throughout the Middle East, North Africa and eventually through Spain into
Central Europe. Relationships with Islam were initially good, with its
general tolerance of Christianity, mutual respect and acceptance of
Christian pilgrimage. Many Christians became Muslims to avoid taxes
from the Byzantine Empire. But although Christianity was spreading
through many lands, in the end the general effect of the Islamic
conquest was to weaken Christianity. A poignant example of the ini-
tial tolerance of Islam towards Christians – a tolerance that would
eventually be shattered – is shown by the story of the peaceful conquest
of Jerusalem by Caliph Omar the Just and the keys to the Church of
the Holy Sepulchre. As Toine van Teeffelen, a Bethlehem-based anthropologist, relates:

> Ironically, the responsibility for guarding the Church of the Holy
> Sepulchre, one of the holiest sites in Christendom, falls on the shoulders
> of two Moslem families, the Joudehs (historically known as Ghudia)
> and the Nusseibehs. According to a complicated agreement whose origins
> are lost in the mists of time, the Joudeh family keeps the keys and the
> Nusseibeh family opens the doors . . . the responsibility has been passed
> from fathers to sons.[8]

Caliph Omar's respect for the church was also shown by the fact that
he refused to pray in it – because then the Muslims might have turned
it into a mosque.[9] Under Muslim rule, despite the merciful behaviour
of Salah-ed-din (Saladin) and his successor, his nephew Kamil (Salah-
ed-din died in 1193), tolerance was interspersed with persecution of
Christians and Jews. In fact, attacks on the holy shrines were one
of the causes of the Crusades. Yet amid this bitterness there is still
one remarkable legend displaying mutual understanding between
St Francis of Assisi and Islam. Francis had joined the Fourth Crusade,
and seeing that the attack was going badly, courageously crossed the
enemy lines to confront Kamil. His intentions were to convert the
Muslim ruler to Christianity, apparently unaware that Kamil was surrounded with Coptic advisers fully familiar with the Christian faith.
St Francis offered to enter a fiery furnace on the condition that should
he come out alive, Kamil and his people would embrace Christianity.

The Sultan replied to the saint with a lesson in humanity and common sense, saying that gambling with one's life was not a valid proof of one's God, and then saw St Francis on his way with courtesy and lavish gifts.

Any hopes of the tolerance and amicable relations between Christianity and Islam continuing were shattered by the Crusades from the eleventh century onward. The slaughter of this period is well documented. The Crusaders – Western Christians – saw Muslims, Jews and Eastern Christians all as enemies. From this tragic period, antagonism between Eastern and Western Christians has been the legacy, although the many movements of reconciliation have begun to rebuild trust – the Middle East Council of Churches is now the most ecumenical body in the world.[10]

Relationships with Islam remain extremely complex. Palestine, between 1517 and 1917, was ruled by the Ottoman Empire, and the Churches played an important role in providing material help – medical, food and education – to an impoverished population. But whereas the relationship with the rulers was tense and difficult (the genocide of Armenian Christians should never be forgotten), frequently at village level relationships between Muslim and Christian were positive, a fact frequently stressed today. So it must be stated clearly that, even in a global, post-September 11 context of the American so-called 'war against terror' (a phrase now widely discredited in the current US Presidency of Barack Obama), the frequent unjust targeting and scapegoating of Muslims as terrorists, the cruel false assumption that Arabs are all Muslims and terrorists – despite all this, normally relationships between Christians and Muslims in Palestine are amicable. Of course there are disputes – as there are with all groups of people. The late husband of Jean Zaru (a Quaker theologian and activist who lives in Ramallah in the West Bank), was principal of the Quaker School at Ramallah for 18 years. The students at this school were mainly Muslim, and Jean Zaru is explicit about the good relations between the two groups and the fact that Christians, who are in a minority, have learned to coexist with their fellow Muslims.[11] That there are extremist groups of violence cannot be denied; but the focus in this book will be the groups – here and elsewhere – that have chosen to work for peace non-violently and in a holistic manner.

A more recent significant historical factor for Christians in the Holy Lands was the Protestant missionary movement preceding, accompanying and following the colonialist movements of the nineteenth century. This would provide yet another means of dividing Christians. It is frequently assumed that Palestinian Christians are all converts as a result of this movement. Yet as Sami Awad, director of the Holy Land Trust in Bethlehem, declared on being asked if he was a convert from Islam to Christianity: 'Yes, I am a convert: my ancestors converted at Pentecost!'[12] His declaration highlights what causes Christians in the Middle East frequent suffering: that they are the successors of the first Christians and seldom recognized as such.

The last factor that needs to be addressed in bridging the centuries with the first Christians and providing the most significant precursor to the current scene was the development of Christian Zionism, especially in the nineteenth century. In fact this had much earlier roots, which actually preceded and encouraged Jewish Zionism, in the Protestant Reformation and subsequent thinking in the sixteenth and seventeenth centuries.[13] It was John Nelson Darby (1800–82), founder of the Plymouth Brethren, who laid the foundations of Evangelical Christian Zionism. He built a bridge between biblical prophecy and its historical development, dividing history into seven epochs or 'dispensations', culminating in the millennial kingdom of Jesus, following the battle of Armageddon. Here the inspiration was not the four Gospels, but Revelation. Darby's popularity waned in Britain and he then concentrated his Dispensationalism on America – with immense consequences for today's developments.

The way that Christian Zionism was able to coincide with the aims of Jewish Zionism attained its culminating moment in the founding of the State of Israel on 14 May 1948.[14] Many Christians were convinced that a homeland should be restored to the Jewish people long before the Shoah (Holocaust). In Britain, Lord Shaftesbury was a key actor in this movement. A friend of Lord Balfour, with his passionate philanthropy, Lord Shaftesbury combined a fervent evangelicalism, adhering to the belief that the Second Coming of Christ would take place in Israel, which must become the homeland for the Jews (although other places, such as Cyprus and Uganda, had been proposed). The idea of 'The ingathering of Jews', which must be made possible for Christ's coming, continues to fuel both Christian and Jewish Zionism.[15]

Such passion for Israel's restoration on the part of Christian evangelicals coincided with Theodore Herzl's call for a Jewish state that would be 'an outpost in the heart of darkness'. Herzl (1860–1904), who was born in Budapest and active in Vienna, was responsible for the first Zionist Congress in Basel (Switzerland) in 1897. He pleaded: 'When will it seem that my efforts on this earth have been successful? When poor Jewish boys become proud young Jews.'[16]

But this could not happen without a country, as Herzl expressed in *Der Judenstaat* in 1896.[17] The racism of Herzl's attitude – the despising of the indigenous population of Palestine – has been compared by the late Michael Prior to the conquest of South Africa by the British and Dutch, and the North American conquest of indigenous Indians.[18] He points out that it is a racism that has extended into the present. For example, the famous biblical archaeologist, William Foxwell Albright, stated:

> From the standpoint of a philosopher of history, it often seems *necessary that a people of marked inferior type, should vanish before a people of superior potentialities, since there is a point beyond which racial mixture cannot go without disaster* ... Thus the Canaanites with their orgiastic nature worship, their cult of fertility in the form of serpent symbols and sensuous nudity, and their gross mythology, were replaced by Israel, with its pastoral simplicity and purity of life, its lofty monotheism and its severe code of ethics.[19]

Herzl's Zionist movement, originally a secular Jewish movement, was violently opposed by Jewish Orthodoxy: for it was their profound belief that the Messiah, not human beings, would restore the land of Israel. Such an act required divine intervention. But Herzl thought Jews would never be respected without a country, and sought a European sponsor for his project. Gradually this secular movement became transformed into a Jewish religious movement, especially by the efforts of Rabbi Avraham Yitzchak Kook (1865–1935) and later his son. Rabbi Kook came to Israel in 1904 and his teachings 'integrated the traditional, passive religious longing for the land with the modern, secular, active Zionism, giving birth to a comprehensive, religious-nationalist ideology'.[20] The Rabbi saw this form of utopian Zionism as the means not only of restoring Jews to the Holy Land, but also of redemption for the whole of humanity. He even saw the Balfour Declaration[21] as divinely inspired. But it was his son, Rabbi Zvi Yehuda Kook, who, in the wake of the 1967 Arab–Israeli War, mediated his father's teachings, and was responsible for his becoming a cult hero and inspiration for the *Gush Emunim* settler movement in the developing State of Israel.

Nor was it coincidental that there should be a change in the fortunes of Jews worldwide. Expelled from Jerusalem by the Romans in 70 AD, they had been a minority in Palestine under Islam and endured discrimination and anti-Semitism from Christians, an anti-Semitism that would spread throughout Europe, bursting out in expulsions and pogroms and culminating in the persecution and Holocaust of Hitler's Nazi Germany. The memory of this suffering is a constant strand in this book. What had sparked Jewish nationalism in the nineteenth century was the French Revolution – as it had sparked other contemporary nationalist movements. Hence Zionism was originally conceived as a secular, colonialist movement. But finally, in Lord Balfour was found a European sponsor – although, ironically, Balfour's enthusiasm was founded on his reading of the Bible. At the same time pressure had been building up in America for the return of the Jews to Palestine. For example, William Blackstone, a Methodist and ardent believer that the true home of the Jews was Israel, had written to President Benjamin Harrison, supporting this cause.[22] Significantly, in 1922, Britain obtained the Mandate for Palestine, eventually to be handed over to the United Nations in 1948. Many difficulties and tensions were experienced during the next two decades, including the Arab rebellion of 1936. The Second World War brought the situation to a head. The Jewish people were enduring the systemic persecution of the Hitler regime and feared total extermination. Many Jews wanted to go to the United States, but the Zionists wanted them to be part of the new Palestine. So now came the fateful partition of the land by the United Nations: the Israelis were given 56 per cent and the Palestinians were given 44 per cent. When the British left, the Israelis officially declared the State of Israel. According to Naim Ateek, 'the Palestinians paid the price for European anti-Semitism'.[23] We are thus confronted by an immense chasm and a complex situation dividing us from the earliest followers of Jesus and the challenges of the first Christians of the Bible lands.

Contemporary tensions

The truth is that two peoples claim the same land. And they claim it with an intensity and love that constitutes their very identity. This has often been taught to biblical students in the West in a very one-sided way. In my own theological studies, in the context of post-Holocaust sympathy for the Jewish people and the attempt to eradicate anti-Semitism in Christian theology, the stress was placed on Jewish love for *ha arets* (the land), and the evidence of this in Scripture was easy to find. Many biblical scholars of this period attempted to redress the wrongs of the Jewish people through European history, but in a way that was blind to the existence and history of the Palestinian people. So it was a revelation – and part of 'the water flowing from the other side of the mountain' (the phrase of the biblical scholar Kenneth Bailey)[24] – to discover an equal passion for the land among Arab Christians and Muslims. Anyone reading Elias Chacour's book (Elias Chacour is Archbishop of Galilee), *We Belong to the Land*, cannot fail to be overwhelmed by the tremendous affinity with the land he expresses – the trees, rocks and landscapes of Palestine.

> Mobile western people have difficulty comprehending the significance of the land for Palestinians. We belong to the land. We identify with the land, which has been treasured, cultivated, and nurtured by countless generations of ancestors. As a child I joined my family in moving large rocks from the fields ... It took months to clear the stones from just a small field. The land is so holy, so sacred to us, because we have given it our sweat and blood.[25]

Many such stories lament the lost trees and plants, and the farmers' lost livelihood of tending to olive and fruit trees.

Tragically for the indigenous population, the division of the territory of Palestine proposed by the United Nations was never honoured, as the Zionist government took 78 per cent of the land, not 56 per cent (see page 9), even though there were far more Palestinian inhabitants than Jewish. Thousands of Palestinians were pushed out of what is now Israel, so that only the West Bank and Gaza (22 per cent) were left to Palestinians – Muslims and Christians. In 1967 a war was fought between Egypt and Syria on the one hand and Israel on the other. Jordan, who was in control of the West Bank and East Jerusalem at that time, joined the war and lost all of the 22 per cent that remained of Palestine. Arab countries – Syria, Jordan and Egypt, with contributions from others – invaded to help Palestine but were ultimately no match for the might of the Israeli armed forces. At this point, between 750,000 and 800,000 people were driven from their homes in what has been called by the Israeli historian, Ilan Pappé, the ethnic cleansing of Palestine, and described by the Arabic words *al-Nakba*, 'the catastrophe'.[26]

In this, 531 villages were razed to the ground. A few were left to be taken over by the Jewish people. Those Palestinians who tried to return after the armistice were killed. There were four million refugees – many in camps to this day in Palestine, Jordan and Lebanon – with no right of return to their homes. There are now 1.5 million Palestinians in Gaza, 2.5 million in the West Bank and 1.3 million inside Israel.[27] But the situation constantly changes, given the increasing level of harassment in the three areas.

Whereas Christianity had been the dominant religion until Crusader times, Christians now make up less than 2 per cent of the population. There are 400,000 Palestinian Christians in the world, 50,000 in Palestine and 110,507 in Israel.[28] Those who live in Israel, while facing restrictions and difficulties, experience far fewer difficulties than those in the West Bank, who live under Israeli occupation, suffer poverty, daily harassment and persecution.

Naim Ateek's predictions are stark for the future of Christianity in the Bible lands.[29] Because there is no real movement in the peace process, and the oppression gets steadily worse, Christians in Gaza will gradually disappear, the West Bank will lose its Christian presence in the north and the remaining Christians will cluster in the south around the Ramallah and Bethlehem areas. In Bethlehem only 1.5 per cent of the population is now Christian – such is the effect of emigration. There is no reason for those who emigrated to return, given economic and political instability. The vitality and very viability of

Christian life will depend on the ending of the occupation and establishment of a democratic state, whether this be a one- or two-state solution. Only then can there be realistic hopes of return to the lost land and villages.

Keep the Holy Land holy – the role of the worldwide Christian community

No wonder that Palestinian Christians desperately need the solidarity of the wider Christian world and Churches in order to survive. Naim Ateek called for Christians to be helped in order to stay in the land. The former Latin patriarch, Michel Sabbah, put it even more strongly: 'Every Christian has a vocation for the Holy Land – to keep it holy and as a place of redemption. This is an obligation for every Christian and every Church.'[30] On this occasion, in 2006, he even declared that Israel needed help to be able to make peace, *since Israel has lost its soul, the true soul of Israel.* The same appeal was made by Archbishop Desmond Tutu to the Jewish people when he was speaking at a Friends of Sabeel Conference in Boston. Realizing that Jews in the USA felt impregnable because of the might of America's backing, he recalled them to the heart of Torah and the Prophets, where God is on the side of the oppressed and they were continually reminded of the need to care for the stranger, the widow and the orphan, 'because you were sojourners in Egypt':

> 'Remembering what happened to you in Egypt and much more recently in Germany – remember, and act appropriately,' he said, alluding to the enslavement of Jews in Egypt described in the book of Exodus, as well as to the Nazi Holocaust. 'If you reject your calling, you may survive for a long time, but you will find it is all corrosive inside, and one day you will implode.'[31]

Advent's quest: a praxis of reconciliation

Given this troubled history, only summarily sketched here, what kind of illumination can the rereading of the Gospels furnish for the Advent journey seeking peace? One clue that the Christmas feast provides is in its connection with *gift-giving.* I began with an allusion to the addictive patterns of consumption that the secular celebration of Christmas encourages. A familiar practice of giving. But if a reading of the Gospels in an Advent journey could illuminate a deeper form of giving that leads to *forgiving*, this could truly open up what I call a *praxis of reconciliation*. It is a praxis, not merely a goal, because it is a form of *reflective action* involving *conversion and testing of the heart's integrity, that will challenge every aspect of living*.[32]

A praxis of reconciliation will combine many ingredients: peace with justice requires, first, mercy and a commitment to truth, leading to repentance and forgiveness. These seek as a prerequisite the building of trust and empathy – *the willingness to inhabit the space of the other*. Where Christian Churches are concerned, there is a real need for the healing of mistrust and a moving on from the wounds and splits of the past. In the Bible lands and in the Middle East as a whole, spreading to Iraq and Afghanistan and back to the streets of Britain, there is also an urgent need for a more meaningful dialogue with Islam, drawing on positive memories of peaceful coexistence, resources of shared traditions and the importance of prayer, concern for poor people and desire for peace. This dialogue will try to recognize and even inhabit the truth of the other, and will also need to be sensitive to the needs of the Jewish people, their painful history of persecution and need for a homeland.

A praxis of reconciliation will focus on the longings for peace and struggle for justice of all peoples in conflict situations in a holistic manner; it will respect people's need for survival with dignity, for a life that allows the celebration of culture and festival, and that respects tradition and memories. It will also address the longing for inner peace in each person's heart.

But how are we to do this as we move through Advent to Christmas? Let us begin the journey where the Gospels chose to begin – with the prophet and witness, John the Baptizer. His birth, like that of Jesus, was miraculous and foretold by an angel; he too met a violent death. He is the one going before us, journeying into the desert, opening up the journey to repentance, the clarion call to set out, hearts set on beholding the Advent vision of reconciled Creation.

1

John the Baptist – prophet of the Advent journey

And you, child, will be called the prophet of the Most High.

(Luke 1.76)

The way of peace is the way of truth.[1]

Advent's themes of waiting, preparing, longing for the dawn of reconciled creation are presented in all four Gospels, first, by the strange,
austere and prophetic figure of John, son of Zechariah, called 'Baptizer'
by the Synoptic Gospels and 'witness' by the Gospel of John. What
could be the role of John in our journey? Is he depicted in the Gospels
only as precursor, eclipsed by his far more famous cousin, forgotten
after his brutal beheading by Herod Antipas? Or is there more to
discover about his prophetic role that could inspire our quest? Mindful
of the tendency of Christian tradition, already glimpsed in John's
Gospel, to downplay John the Baptist's importance in comparison
with Jesus', let us try to uncover John's distinctive role. Through John
the theme of non-violent resistance will be introduced, and the centuries will be bridged from John's ascetic life in the desert to the
contemporary situation of the Negev desert today and the urgent
need for reconciliation with the earth as part of a holistic journey to
reconciliation. Who are the 'John the Baptists' today, we ask, in the
struggle for justice over land and water? What is his contemporary
message for us now, where, in the West, we generally have abundance
of water and overuse or misuse land in a variety of ways, and where,
in the Middle East, water is scarce and land a bitter source of conflict?
I shall explore how John's spirituality of repentance is both the first
step, and yet an enduring summons on this Advent journey.

A miraculous birth

Only in Luke's Gospel are we given a few precious historical nuggets about the birth of John, even if these function mostly as a frame for the birth of Jesus.[2] The story of John, son of Zechariah, a priest active in the Temple, and Elizabeth, elderly and living under the stigma of childlessness – still an area of suffering for poor women in many countries today – suggests that John's emerging type of prophecy will not be easy to categorize. He is the son of a priest, yet he will not be active in the Temple. Like Jesus, his birth is foretold by an angel, Gabriel, and the second Annunciation (to Mary) has been the source of an inspirational art tradition that has acquired a vibrant life of its own. Also like Jesus, he will die a violent death, as innocent victim. Central figures of this first chapter of Luke – and prefiguring his concern for women throughout the Gospel – are two female figures, the aging Elizabeth and the young, unmarried Mary. In the case of John, the role of the Holy Spirit in his life is made clear, as is John's vocation to be in 'the spirit and power of Elijah' (Luke 1.17). Elijah will further inspire the kind of prophet this child will become as he will be thought of as a returning Elijah. His ascetic vocation is a striking feature, and one that offers another kind of prophetic action for our situation. It is common to compare the promised miraculous births – particularly that of John – with the promise and birth of the prophet Samuel to his mother Hannah (1 Sam. 1–28; 2.1–11). But there are other memories to evoke: one is the promise of the birth of Ishmael to Hagar, in the difficult context of the relationship between Sarah (also, like Elizabeth, childless) and Abraham (Gen. 16.1–5; 21.1–21). Hagar is an important figure for womanist (African-American women) theologians and black-led churches; her son, Ishmael, is crucial to Islam. They too evoke the desert context that will be crucial to the story of John. Nor should we forget Rachel, who died giving birth to the baby Benoni ('son of my sorrow') on the way to Bethlehem (Gen. 35.16–21) and whose tomb there is so important for Jewish pilgrimage (though now cut off for Christians and Muslims).

John is thought to have been born at Ein Kerem, 'the gracious spring', below Mount Orah, a village four kilometres west of Jerusalem.

In 1106 his birthplace was discovered by the Crusader Daniel to be in a cave, now within the Franciscan Church of St John.

This apparently tranquil village has, more recently, experienced a troubled history. In 1944–5 it had a population of 3,180. The UN Partition Plan for the new State of Israel in 1947 placed Ein Kerem in the Jerusalem enclave intended for international control. But after the April 1948 massacre at the nearby village of Deir Yassin, most of the women and children in the village were evacuated. The village was then attacked by Israeli forces during the ten-day truce of July 1948, and the remaining civilian inhabitants fled. The Arab forces, which had been encamped in the village, also left after Israeli troops had captured two hilltops dominating Ein Kerem and shelled the village. During its last days the people of Ein Kerem suffered from very severe food shortages. Israel later incorporated the village into the municipal boundaries of Jerusalem. Yet Ein Kerem was one of the few depopulated Arab localities to survive the war with most of its buildings intact – but without its Arab citizens. Jewish immigrants, mainly from Yemen, moved into the emptied homes, though over the years the pleasant rural atmosphere attracted a population of Jewish artisans and craftsmen. The Sisters of Sion have made Ein Kerem the centre for their work of Jewish–Christian relations.

Such was the more recent history of this village, 2,000 years after the biblical Visitation event. Here was the destination of the young Mary of Nazareth, walking across the hills of Judaea from Nazareth to visit her kinswoman, Elizabeth. The site of the Visitation is thought to be on the other side of the valley, now in the Franciscan church: in its crypt is the spring, supposedly the site of their meeting. Above the church, the Russian Convent of Elizabeth rises above the trees on the slopes of Mount Orah.[3]

The climax of the historic encounter of the mothers of John and Jesus was the famous Magnificat (Luke 1.46–55), a prayer that continues to inspire hope in many places of affliction. Traditionally this is Mary's song, but it has been suggested recently by Scripture scholars, such as David Catchpole, that it is more correctly Elizabeth's song as, echoing Hannah, it celebrates God's merciful action in giving her a son and removing the stigma of barrenness.[4] But then what must have happened was that Elizabeth faded from prominence after the birth of John, Mary took centre stage and the prayer remained attributed to her. The final version of the text that we read today after the process of re-editing certainly presents the voice of Mary passionately proclaiming God's liberating actions.

The next event in the unfolding drama is the birth of John (Luke 1.57–66). His father Zechariah's famous prayer, known as the Benedictus, is important in making it crystal clear that John will be a prophet: 'And you, child, will be called the prophet of the Most High' (Luke 1.76). But even more vitally, and echoing the prophet Isaiah (9.2), John's role will be to make us ready for when the day shall dawn upon us from on high, 'to give light to those who sit in darkness and in the shadow of death, to guide our feet into the way of peace' (1.79). This is the inspiration of John for the Advent and Christmas journey: he brings hope that following his footsteps, asking how his prophecy speaks to us today, not only our feet but also our hearts will turn towards the task of peacemaking and reconciliation.

A prophet of repentance and righteousness

Why did John flee to the desert? The Synoptic Gospels give him the role of 'preparing the way' for Jesus, and we are familiar with this ministry. Only Luke tells us that 'the child grew and became strong in spirit, and he was in the wilderness until the day of his public appearance to Israel' (1.80).

Both Matthew and Mark also depict him as preaching repentance in the wilderness (Matt. 3.1; Mark 1.4), and John as being sent to bear witness to the light, but not himself being the light (John 1.6–8) – seemingly John the Baptizer is already being downplayed in significance compared with Jesus. All three Synoptic Gospels identify John the Baptist as the figure foretold by Isaiah, 'the voice of him that crieth in the wilderness' (Isa. 40.3; AV), as 'my messenger . . . who will prepare your way' (Luke 7.27) – although this is actually the prophecy of Malachi (3.1) in the context of ushering in the judgement of the end times: 'But who can endure the day of his coming . . . ?' (3.2) – the poignant question, so beautifully put to music in Handel's *Messiah*. This gives us the first clue that John has a role independent

of Jesus, to point to the end times and the fulfilment of God's promise: *the heart of Advent's message.*

That John is a prophet in the Elijah tradition is indisputable.
Malachi has already prophesied that 'I will send you Elijah the prophet
before the great and awesome day' (Mal. 4.5). Luke tells us that:

> ... he will go before him in the spirit and power of Elijah, to turn
> the hearts of the fathers to the children, and the disobedient to the
> wisdom of the just, to make ready for the Lord a people prepared.
>
> (Luke 1.17)

If we see 'The Lord' as God, not Jesus, this again stresses John's role,
like Elijah's, as being to call a community, already under threat, to
repent, to embrace righteousness, in readiness for the end times.
As David Catchpole writes: 'His mission is to bring about changes of
heart and life, especially the healing of inter-generational discord and
conflict, which are the first priority in the face of terror.'[5]

Again, like Elijah's flight from the court of Ahab, John goes to the
desert, as Jesus himself would do, and as did many groups of his time,
such as the Essenes of the Qumran community. So now we explore
the two questions of, first, the poverty issues faced by the people of
John's time and, second, what this desert of his day was, and what it
has now become.

Poverty in New Testament times

John the Baptist's poverty was a self-chosen radical asceticism, a
voluntary renunciation: tradition has it that he was a Nazirite, consecrated to God and asked to bear witness through this lifestyle.

In John's time, the Jewish communities of Judaea were largely
composed of poor people, exploited by corrupt rulers and wealthy
landowners, both Jewish and Roman. Most scholars admit that the
poverty of the majority of the Jewish population at the time of Jesus
was due to the exploitation of the Roman occupation.[6] Commenting
on the uniquely Lukan story of the lost coin (Luke 15.8–10), where the
value of the coin was equal to one denarius, Luise Schottroff explains
that this was the daily wage that the worker in the vineyard would
expect – and he would not be in regular work. Two hundred denarii

was the average *yearly* income of a worker on the land. This would not have been sufficient to sustain his family even in bread. So there must have been small plots of land – where women and children also worked (children were expected to work from the age of six).[7] Women worked also in textile production as weavers, but in both cases they earned less than men. So the point of the story of the lost coin is that the woman had lost the equivalent of a labourer's daily wage, for which she had worked harder and longer to get. One of the problems of getting an accurate picture of the poverty of both women and men is the comparative invisibility of women's work. The Gospels speak of fisher*men* but not fisher*women*. Yet in all the fishing communities I know, both in the West and in the East, women are at the centre of the work, mending nets, sorting, cleaning and selling fish. Many cultures forbid their entering the sea for reasons of pollution.

Poverty is measured in terms of hunger, housing, poor clothing – and the misery of debt that forced people into slavery. The social stigma attached to many trades is also relevant. In some senses there are parallels between first-century Palestine and contemporary rural Rajasthan (north-west India). In the poor communities I know well, people are poor through a mixture of the harsh conditions of the desert, experiencing both drought and floods, caste-based poverty, the consequences of colonization and unjust local rulers as well as the dangers of racial violence or bandits.[8] The robbers on the road to Jericho come to mind. Failure of the harvest brings famine and overreliance on the money lender: because debt spirals out of control, people are forced to sell themselves as bonded labourers for a lifetime, even passing on the debt to their children. It is no accident that all the Synoptic Gospels tell many stories about debt. In the first century, dung collectors and tanners were also despised, because of the foul smell connected with their activities. If a woman was married to either one of these, she had the right to claim divorce.[9] This recalls the current despising of Dalits (formerly given the disparaging term 'Untouchables') in India, especially because they skin dead cows and clean latrines. The parallel is important as it shows that the inability of poor people to move out of poverty is linked not just with failure to earn a regular wage, but also with entrenched notions of purity and pollution. Recalling diverse contexts of poverty also uncovers the links between poverty, violence and conflict.

For poor people, simply getting enough to eat was the main problem. Meat was rare – as we see in the parable of the Prodigal Son and the fattened calf (Luke 15.22–24), the elder brother complained that no calf had been killed for him. Poor people could not afford wheat or meat, and ate barley bread. Michael Prior tells us that they were reduced to eating locusts for meat, as well as older domestic animals.[10] This puts John's diet in the desert in context – locusts were his form of protein. In rural Rajasthan, diet is still a huge problem. Most women are undernourished and in consequence are anaemic: many die in childbirth, and the child mortality rate is very high due to poor diet, lack of clean water and no access to medical care. Globally speaking, the UN World Food Programme (2009) has said that over a billion people are going hungry each day: 19 million in Africa are near starvation.[11]

The non-existence of medical care for poor people in the time of Jesus – they could not have afforded the 'doctors' of their day – is part of the reason that the sick flocked to Jesus in hope of healing. But the biggest contrast between rich and poor is in terms of security. The rich can afford to prepare for the lean years by storing grain in barns. Their houses are proof against storms and floods. They wear clothing both beautiful and warm – as we see from the parable of Dives and Lazarus (Luke 16.19–21). Contrast the poor men I see on the streets of Delhi every year (admittedly this is a city, not a village – it is easier to find hospitality and shelter in a village): it is winter, and they are huddled on the pavements around a small fire built from a few sticks. They pull their cloaks around them to shut out the wind, and try to boil a small pan to make some warm tea (chai). Or take the villages, where the peoples' small huts are normally adequate to provide shelter – but not in a storm or when rivers burst their banks: then they are swept away as easily as a child's house of paper. Of course these parallels are not exact, but they evoke the harsh realities of poverty in *all* times. Here they are described to paint a picture of the injustices of the time and to show why John felt strongly that God's righteousness was so absent that he felt called to leave normal society for self-chosen asceticism in the desert.

The Negev Desert – then and now

The desert where John dwelt was the Negev Desert, which covers more than half of Israel; that is, it extends over some 13,000 km² (4,700 sq. miles), or at least 55 per cent of the country's land area. It forms an inverted triangle shape whose western side is contiguous with the desert of the Sinai Peninsula, and whose eastern border is the Arabah Valley. It is a rocky desert, a mixture of brown, rocky, dusty mountains interrupted by wadis (dry riverbeds that bloom briefly after rain) and deep craters. Ecologically it covers five different regions: northern, western and central Negev, the high plateau and the Arabah Valley. These differ in terms of rainfall, from the Mediterranean zone, with adequate rain, to the high plateau area of the Negev Heights, which gets only 100 mm of rain per year and has inferior and partly salty soils. The Arabah Valley, which stretches 180 km from Eilat in the south to the tip of the Dead Sea in the north, is very arid, with barely 50 mm of rain annually. Its soil is inferior, and little can grow without irrigation and special soil additives.

These bare facts about the Negev say nothing about its significance to the peoples who live there. As the writers of *The Negev: The Challenge of a Desert* say:

> It is no whim of history that the birth of the first monotheistic faith took place in a desert, or that it was followed by the other two great religions, Christianity and Islam. The prophets of Israel repeatedly sought and found inspiration in the desert, Christian hermits fled to it to escape the pollution of the world, and to commune with God, and in modern times the secular literature of the desert ... reveals the powerful influence it exerts on the minds and spirits of all who seek its mysteries.[12]

There is a special magic about deserts, as I know from my experiences in the desert of Rajasthan. The creatures of the desert – birds, deer and wilder animals – are at home in a way that humans are not. Distances are overwhelming. The fear of being lost is always a threat. And yet if John lived there for some time, he must have become well acquainted with small tracks, with water sources, with trees giving some small shelter against winds and sandstorms, and with the places where desert plants giving nourishment could grow. John's diet of 'locusts and wild honey' should not be seen as a sign of eccentricity, rather as an indication of his *disciplined ability to live on the sustenance the desert provided.*

Above all, if dwelling in the desert was a way of experiencing the presence of God in an intense manner (for Jesus too), it is helpful to evoke why this could be so:

> It is night in the desert. After a blazing day in the windswept emptiness, the dark brings relief to the aching body, parched by heat. Enormous stars hang low over the dustless, dry atmosphere. Nothing stirs. The absolute silence is tangible, audible. Here are no whispering trees, no veils of cloud, no grassy meadows for the disporting of gods and goddesses. Here is that 'voice of stillness' in which God spoke to his prophet Elijah. Here, in this silent world, not soft, not gentle, in this awesome boundlessness of time and space, one man stands alone, touched by infinity.[13]

This is the place in which John chose to discipline himself and shape his calling to be a prophet of repentance for the end times.

The desert and the water shortage – today's realities

For John, as for desert people today, the cry is 'Water!', and the reality, in these days of global warming and climate change, is that water is a precious resource that is shrinking on a global scale.

John the Baptist summoned the people of his day to repentance – but what would the issues be for conversion in contemporary times? The reality is that, yes, water issues are critical for Israel, but far more severe, even life-threatening, in the West Bank and Gaza, where all Christians and Muslims are caught up in the suffering and injustice of the Israeli occupation. This section attempts an overview of some areas: whereas in the narrative of poverty of the first century, we saw the focus was on food, clothing, housing and the curing of serious illness and disability, the focus today is more strikingly on issues of water and land, but also on food and housing. Lack of water – and poor quality of water – are now recognized globally as the most important causes of poor health, illness and child mortality. Three million children die from dysentery every year – six thousand a day from waterborne diseases such as gastro-enteritis. Some 8 per cent of diseases in the poor Global South are water-related.[14] The infrastructure of water supplies has been almost eradicated in war-torn areas like Afghanistan; it will take more than 20 years to repair and make usable the water sources in post-war Iraq.

Land was also important for John's community, and for Jesus: the Gospels portray Jesus as always on the move, from the Jordan to the desert, to Nazareth, through Galilee's villages and eventually to Jerusalem. We have already seen, in the work of Elias Chacour, how powerful for Palestinians is their love for this same land, tended and dwelt in for over 2,000 years, and noted how this needs to be better understood and recognized as the other side of the coin to the way Jewish people love the land of Israel.

Hwaa Irfan, in a significant article, writes of this

> strong organic relationship . . . between a land and its people generation after generation. The respect for and the understanding of their ecosystem shape their lives. When respected, the environment is the source of well-being, but when abused it becomes the source of ill health [sic] and discord.[15]

Palestine, he continues, once covered 26,320 km² of land and 704 km² of inland water. Formerly there were rolling woodlands covered with thickets, forests and grasslands. When the 1948 war displaced between 700,000 and 800,000 Palestinians, this meant a massive influx of refugees into a fragile ecosystem and the beginning of the destruction of over 419 Palestinian villages. By the time of the 1967 Israeli occupation, Gaza was on the brink of a water crisis, with frequent outbreaks of waterborne diseases and increased soil alkalinity and salinity. Palestine is now two separate landmasses: the West Bank and the Gaza Strip, including the Dead Sea, and covering a surface of 6,210 km². Barren hills have now replaced woodlands and deserts have replaced grasslands. Because of the Israeli occupation, expansion, and increased construction projects, Palestine now suffers from a weakened agricultural system, wastewater, solid-waste pollution problems and water security issues.

To look first at the water issue: the Palestinian entitlement to water includes the underground water of the West Bank and Gaza aquifers, and a rightful share as riparians to the Jordan River. Israel uses the Western Aquifer System on the West Bank via three hundred deep underground wells. Palestinians are limited to 22 mcm annually.[16] Palestinians now have roughly 20 per cent access, Israelis 80 per cent.[17] The Gaza Aquifer – the region's only freshwater source – supplies 2,200 wells. Its annual safe yield is 55 mcm, but it is now overpumped at 110 mcm. This lowers the water table below sea level, causing saline water intrusion from the saline strata, seawater and return flows from intensive irrigation. In total, 246 mcm of water supplies 3 million Palestinians for domestic, industrial and agricultural needs, compared with 1,946 mcm of water for 6 million Israelis. From the North-East Aquifer System on the West Bank, Palestinians receive 42 mcm, whereas Israel receives 103 mcm annually. Israel's Minster of Agriculture, Rafael Eitan, has declared on Israeli radio that the country would be in mortal danger if it lost control of this mountain aquifer.[18]

What this unequal distribution means is a deeply distressing, and worsening, water shortage that is especially hard on residents of Palestinian villages that are not connected to a water network. As of June 2006, some 215,000 Palestinians in 220 villages lived in communities without a running-water network. In the winter and autumn, these residents collect rainfall in cisterns next to their homes and use the water for all their needs. In the spring and summer months, when the water in the cistern becomes depleted, residents rely on water from nearby springs and on water brought to them by owners of private water-tankers.

There are also hundreds of thousands of Palestinians who live in communities with a central running-water network that supplies water irregularly, in limited amounts, and does not reach everyone in the community. For this reason, some Palestinian authorities supply water in the summer months on a rotation basis: each neighbourhood receives water once every few days, for one day or several hours at a time. To supplement the water supplied, these residents have to buy water brought to them in privately owned water-tankers. This is a very heavy burden. Per-capita water consumption for household and municipal use in communities connected to a central running-water network in the West Bank is 60 litres a day. *In Israel, per-capita daily use is 280 litres, thus more than 4.5 times greater*. It should be stressed that this situation deteriorates daily in Gaza (especially in a conflict situation, for example, in December 2008), and in summer there are severe shortages in the West Bank – and we have not mentioned the anguish that lack of water causes in, for example, the difficult maintenance of hospitals; or that the Israeli army has recently been destroying water cisterns in the Beqaa valley, so that farmers have no means of irrigating their fruit trees. The heavy cost of having to pay for water means that while the cost of water supplied by a central running-water network ranges from 3 to 5 shekels per cubic metre, the water-tanker owners charge from 15 to 30 shekels per cubic metre, depending on the supplier and the location of the community. With 46 per cent of the residents living under the poverty line and more than 27 per cent of them unemployed, water purchases are a heavy financial burden for a substantial segment of the local population. According to research of the Palestinian Hydrology Group, there are many cases in which water purchases amount to 10 per cent of the family's expenses – where families can afford to buy water. For many, it is too expensive. It is still in Gaza, post-conflict, where the issue is most critical.[19]

Thus many families are forced to reduce their consumption, making it harder for them to meet their basic needs, such as personal hygiene, house cleaning, and dish and clothes washing. Research studies have shown that a shortage of water causes a decline in personal hygiene. Dr Julie Trottier of the Université Catholique de Louvain pointed out that Palestinians only have control of 18 per cent of the available water, and that 60 per cent of that small allowance actually goes towards irrigation under the control of villagers who have regulated their water resources for centuries with tight social control. Many sources see the water situation in Israel/Palestine as a deepening source of conflict and an obstacle to peacemaking:

> If there are not to be further water wars minimum steps are necessary . . . Above all it should be recognised that the crisis is not so much one of supply as of inequitable distribution, complicated by historic grievances, ideological quarrels and questions of national security.[20]

In addition to water, food production is a source of great difficulty for Palestinians. The policy of 'closure' has prevented farmers from reaching the markets, making food more expensive. When they are able to sell their produce they are forced to sell it for a much lower price. The land of many other farmers has been taken, in some cases torched.

Land is crucial to the Palestinian economy, whereas agriculture today accounts for less than 3 per cent of industrialized Israel's GDP.[21] During the Intifada (the Palestinian uprising of 2000), Israeli forces uprooted acres of olive trees, grapevines, palm trees, almonds, oranges, figs, strawberries, guava and bananas. The grief this caused can scarcely be described. Cases of cleared land documented by the Palestinian Ministry of Agriculture show that 271,797 trees have been uprooted. Palestinians now have no sovereignty over, and only limited access to, the region's natural resources.

In addition, most Israeli settlements are built on confiscated Palestinian agricultural or communal grazing lands. Closed military areas, mainly in the Jordan Valley, are located on such land in the West Bank. Also, the overgrazed land available is under threat of permanent desertification. The problems are exacerbated by lack of sewage and wastewater pollution. Many Palestinians are not linked to a sewage system. The wastewater from many Israeli settlements is collected and discharged into nearby valleys without treatment, affecting nearby Palestinian communities. In Nahalin, Bethlehem, for example, the people are exposed to the farm effluents from the nearby Rush Tsorim settlement. Some Israeli settlements in the West Bank are primarily used for cattle and livestock; however, the manure from these farms is dumped in Palestinian valleys and on agricultural lands, destroying soil structure and polluting valuable water resources. This produces a breeding ground for disease. Wastewater from the Ara'el settlement in the Salfiet district flows into a dry creek that is less than 4 m from Salfiet's drinking-water well. This negatively affects both Israelis and Palestinians. In 2008, 30–35 per cent of the agricultural land was severely damaged by wastewater, affecting 400 tons of fruit and the income of the 5,000 inhabitants of Beit Omar. Such examples could be multiplied: this is only *one* picture from *one* country against the global background of environmental devastation in numerous lands. Granted the cherished tradition within Christianity of flight to the desert to seek solitude with God and to protest against the corruption of society, the challenge today is to seek God by tackling all factors causing desertification, degradation of the land and unjust distribution of water.

John's lasting legacy

From his desert fastness John preached repentance for the forgiveness of sins (Mark 1.4), attacked the Pharisees and Sadducees as a 'brood of vipers!' (Matt. 3.7; Luke 3.7) and practised the rite of baptism in the River Jordan as initiation to a life that put conversion into practice and began to show people how the fruits of repentance would blossom. So how does he help us now on our Advent journey? Mindful of the ever-present tendency in spirituality to over-romanticize deserts as chosen places of solitude, in fact desertification as a result of climatic factors is increasing exponentially, causing untold misery to traditional desert dwellers, with consequences also for urban centres.

The first point to establish on this journey to Christmas is how John should be considered in relation to the child of peace. Even if the Gospels see his main significance as preparing the way for, or as witness to Jesus, and find embarrassing the fact that he baptized Jesus, who is clearly far more important, still John is the first beacon of light for Christian communities ready for transformation. People found his appeal relevant and flocked to him. Even the Pharisees apparently did so. Several of Jesus' disciples had been followers of John, whose community continued to exist after Jesus had gone his independent way – probably until his terrible death. Although the theological meaning of baptism would evolve differently, especially as St Paul would teach that it meant being baptized into the death of Jesus, to John we owe the first symbolism of immersion into water as a dramatic sign of conversion and change. John also gave us the setting for the revelation of Jesus as God's beloved son. It was at this moment, too, that Jesus underwent the experience of initiation into his own ministry.[22]

Baptism in the Jordan

The River Jordan (Hebrew: *Yarden*) flows from springs in Mount Hermon to the Sea of Galilee and eventually to the Dead Sea, the lowest place on earth. In many places it forms the boundary between the West Bank and Israel.[23] Yarden is the Israeli officially designated site of Jesus' baptism and today is a highly revered place of pilgrimage. Yet it is probable that John is associated with two baptismal sites: one accessible to the people of Samaria, in the area of Salim,[24] now Tell-er-Ricra, at the five wells of Aenon (the place of the spring), now located at Ed-Der; the other accessible to the people of Judaea, at Bethabara, 'ford-house' or 'ferry-house'.[25] Indeed, Luke has told us that John 'went into all the region around the Jordan' (Luke 3.3). It is likely that Jesus went more than once to John at a Jordan site, and that this is the origin of the two traditions of the meeting at the river.

The baptism of Jesus by John is a major moment of revelation for Jesus of his destiny. Indeed, for the Eastern Churches this moment is celebrated at Epiphany as revelation to the world.[26] The Spirit came upon Jesus and he left his previous calling and went into the desert. Perhaps, subsequently, Jesus felt the need to visit John again (after the Temptations?), and returned to the Jordan, where John reveals that 'This is the one of whom I said, "After me comes a man who ranks before me, because he was before me"' (John 1.30).[27] The spiritual symbolism of water in revealing Jesus as the Spirit of God is not easily captured by Western authors. It is more easily recognized in the East, where the meaning of 'water gives life' is still dynamic. For example, the Indian Christian writer Vandana, in her book *Waters of Life*, uses the Hindu spiritual interest in water to represent 'the true Ganga-ji' (River Ganges) that flows from Jesus' heart, the Spirit, who is both Living Fountain and Fire of Love:

> Waters of Fire is carefully structured into five 'movements of the dance of the waters': waters of recognition (John 1.29–34; 2.1–11), waters of rebirth (3.1–15; 4.1–30); healing waters (5.1–15; 6.16–21); water to drink (7.37–39); and waters of salvation (19.31–37; 21.1–23).[28]

It is the waters that recognize Jesus as Christ, bring about new birth, heal, slake thirst and give salvation. So in this way John's Gospel becomes living water, which is the Spirit, and Jesus is 'The Shining Son of Waters'.[29] So close is the symbolism – Jesus/spirit/water – that highlighting it brings hope of healing to a world where water's deficiency, pollution and mal-distribution have become sources of conflicts and blockages to peace.

John's is a costly witness, faithful until death, leaving us with the memory of a community that confronts the ethics of the time with the urgency of the need for conversion. From Luke we gain the sense of immediacy in the answers John gave to those requiring the specifics of repentance. Those who had more than enough must share food and clothing, tax collectors must not take more than their due and soldiers must not steal violently and must be happy with their pay.[30] It might be said that, even if there is no direct continuity between the two figures, Jesus built his own following on the roots of an earlier community.

And John's ascetic lifestyle, his ability to exist in the utter simplicity of what his environment offered, is an inspiration in this time of planetary crisis. Does he not pronounce judgement over us when we demand food out of season (strawberries all the year round, for example) that is costly in terms of food and air miles and pays unjust wages to those who grow it? Would not John be an advocate today of trade justice movements? I see him as advocating simplicity in our diets, perhaps as a forerunner of the Christian Ecology Link (CEL) and its 'LOAF' principles, which are guides to our shopping and eating habits: these should be based, wherever possible, on what is local, organic, animal-friendly and fairly traded.[31]

Who then are his heirs today? There are ascetics through the centuries in many religious traditions, of course, and most have advocated repentance in the face of a corrupt society. There are also the prophets of creation, like St Francis of Assisi and Hildegard of Bingen. There are two kinds of heirs to John the Baptist. The first are the groups, such as CEL. Given the gravity and possibly ultimately tragic nature of the climatic crisis that threatens to envelop us, the prophetic charism is present most fruitfully in many communities and groups across the religions, and not just in individuals. For example, the Jewish Liberal journal, *Tikkun*, has a strong environmental dimension that includes a critique of Israeli policies in Palestine with regard to water and land settlement.[32] There are Christian communities mushrooming that link healing with working with the land and committing themselves to action for climate change. In Britain, Anglican Church leaders such as the Archbishop of Canterbury, Rowan Williams, the Bishop of London, Richard Chartres and the Bishop of Liverpool, James Jones, have all spoken out directly, urging action for climate change within their own communities and in wider society. The Roman Catholic Church's overseas development agency, CAFOD, is extremely active in a campaign of climate justice – and its networking reaches every Catholic parish.[33]

There are also inspiring prophetic figures across the world urging immediate action, such as the politician Al Gore and the theologian Bill McKibben in the United States, and the late poet/prophet/priest Thomas Berry, proponent of the New Creation Story.[34] It is he above all who has taught us to learn humility about our rightful place in creation. But if I had to choose one recent figure whom I consider to be a John the Baptist figure for contemporary times, it would be Mahatma Gandhi, *the great-souled one.*

Gandhi – prophet, and heir to John the Baptist

At first sight Mohandas Ramchand Gandhi does not seem to be the person we seek. To begin with, he never became a Christian, even though, as we shall see, Gandhi was greatly inspired by the Gospels. He is not strictly speaking contemporary, since he died in January 1948. The political battles he fought – to get the British out of India, to be part of the task of creating a new India and to resist partition – are far from John's concerns. And yet in contrast to prophetic figures such as Thomas Berry, who did not go into the desert to embody their concerns for simplicity, Gandhi's entire life engaged with a radical simplicity that he hoped would set a pattern for the whole country. Not only will I argue here that he is in some sense an heir to John, but in his concern for peace obtained through non-violent means he is also a prophetic Christlike figure.[35]

In his austerity there was a harshness that recalled John the Baptist's asceticism. If John is ridiculed for appearing in a hair shirt, Gandhi, in his simple cotton dhoti[36] on the steps of the British Parliament, was mocked by Winston Churchill as a *naked fakir*. Adopting the traditional dress of peasants was not just part of Gandhi's preferred option of simplicity; it was an attempt to bring cotton-spinning into the home, as part of a renewed economy that would make the villages self-sufficient as far as possible. Gandhi advocated spinning in every household every day, and set an example himself each morning. It was also part of his policy of empowering women by making what we would now call a 'cottage industry' – a way of helping poor women to earn a living. Like John's protest against unjust society, Gandhi's methods were not only directed against the British but against the chosen policies of his own government, especially of Nehru, the first Prime Minster of independent India, which were to develop and industrialize India, thus neglecting the infrastructure of the village. And in Gandhi's own day, most of the people of India dwelt in villages.[37] Even present-day Gandhians, practising simplicity, being strictly vegetarians and working for peace, offer a moral alternative to what is termed 'Shining India' – or the way that India has enthusiastically embraced the policies of global capitalism, preferring large-scale modernization schemes over small-scale grassroots projects, and has continued to neglect the needs of the villages, especially the plight of the poor farmers.[38] Gandhi tried to bring ethics back into economics in a prophetic manner.

Gandhi's ashrams were the places where his ideas took root. Possessions were held in common. Even the most menial work – such as cleaning the toilets – was shared. This was how Gandhi tackled the scourge of Untouchability, the scandal of the way those who were considered outcastes to the Hindu caste system were treated. His diet was extremely simple and, like John, his fasting even unto death in support of his ideals – the composition of the new Constitution[39] and his opposition to the partition of India – was truly heroic. Like both John and Jesus, Gandhi was radical and uncompromising. In his non-violent style of resistance to the injustice and violence of the times, in offering an alternative way of living, he was more Christlike than a John the Baptist figure – as we shall see later.

With the hope that the radicality of John's prophecy is still flourishing today, the Advent journey has begun. Even if today, in many places, the River Jordan is little more than a trickle, it can still evoke the memory of the fiery prophet's words and turn our hearts towards the need for conversion to the earth's needs today; towards working for just distribution of land and water. His urgency evokes the real urgency of commitment to reducing our own carbon footprint, before it is too late. The call to prepare can now be understood as not only preparing for Christmas, but for Advent's longing for the dawn of new creation. John's role is an eschatological one that has a striking relevance to the environmental crisis today: there will be no earth, no planet, no means of avoiding destruction, apocalyptic or not, if we do not heed his call for repentance, conversion and taking responsibility for justice for our threatened planet.

2

The Annunciation

O radiance, radiance of morning's new dawn,
O speak not a word, lest you miss what is born
From the womb of the Godhead creating with pain,
The nourishing gifts of the earth's fruit and grain.

'Is there one here who is hearing?' God's heartbeat is pleading.
She is listening, listening, the bread she is kneading,
The silence enfolds her, deep-hidden its power,
O daughter, beloved, know this is the hour!

O deep is the yearning, for healing she longs
For a people's deliverance from oppression and wrongs.
While moulding the loaf — wheaten flour which earth yields,
She connects with her sisters still toiling in fields.

O daughter, beloved, I heard Rachel's cries,
For the vulnerable children who forever will die
Through the violence of culture, my compassion will stream,
in your waiting, responding, lies my hope and my dream.

O strong is the spirit, insistent and wild,
Evoking response 'I am Wisdom's child!
Let my body, my life, as love's gift remain
For God and my people, for all children in pain.'

The silence is broken, there is rushing of wings,
The cry of the wild goose, exultant it sings –
'O rise up, daughter, love's power will unfold,
Revealing the healing of stories untold.'[1]

Introduction: the Chapel of the Annunciation, Nazareth

It is a piercingly bright sunny morning and the air is crisp and cold. I am sitting in a coffee shop directly opposite the Basilica of the Annunciation in Nazareth. Nazareth is known as the Flower of Galilee, a centre for Christian pilgrimage since the fourth century. The poem above tries to capture some of the prophetic and dynamic character of Annunciation, moving from the mystery of deep contemplation between Mary and the Angel that results in Mary's prophetic action.

The pungent aroma of Turkish coffee mingles with the smell of oriental spices and incense sold in nearby tourist shops: it is impossible not to be excited by the sight of throngs of bustling pilgrims and to try to breathe in the significance of this place and multi-layered shrine. There was once an early Crusader church here, with a Byzantine church lying underneath (thought to be the inspiration of the Empress Helena, mother of Constantine). It was in this church that Christians took shelter during attacks from Muslims. They were all slaughtered and the church was eventually razed to the ground in 1263 by the ferocious Sultan Beybars. Nazareth then became almost a ruin. Eventually the Franciscans gained control of the site of the Annunciation but were themselves expelled in the seventeenth century. The new church, begun in 1871 by the Franciscans, was enlarged and then was itself demolished to make way for the present modern church, on two levels, built on Crusader foundations and consecrated in 1969.

It is the lower church, with its simple Chapel of the Annunciation, claimed to be the site of the home of Mary, which is more evocative and conducive to meditation, even if the actual site of the Annunciation is disputed. It is to this shrine, the heart of the Nazareth New Testament story, that I made my way.[2]

This chapter moves the geography of our Advent journey from Ein Kerem, the River Jordan and the Negev Desert, to the town of Nazareth, significant in the life of Jesus as the site of the Angel Gabriel's Annunciation to Mary of Nazareth, and the site of his early, mostly unknown life, until he began his ministry on the shores of Lake Galilee. So we begin, first, by asking 'Why Nazareth – of what importance was it then and is it now? Second, we shall meditate on Mary's response to Gabriel, integrating it with our peace-seeking journey. An accompaniment of war is usually violence against women, and we shall reflect on Mary as a double symbol of both vulnerability and strength, strikingly mirroring female vulnerability in conflict situations. A focus on the Holy Spirit's role in the story will lead from the dynamics of mutual relation to an investigation into the Spirit's role in inspiring forgiveness and reconciliation, beginning with ourselves. This will lead us to a reflection on Mary's spirituality of contemplation as a life-stance in our personal journey towards peace this Christmas and beyond.

'Can anything good come out of Nazareth?'[3]

Despite this being a cherished holy place for Christian pilgrims, Nazareth does not have a good press. Not only did its inhabitants try to throw Jesus over the cliff (according to Luke 4.29–30), but he was not able to perform miracles here, because of the lack of faith of its inhabitants. It was from the context of Nazareth that we got the saying, 'A prophet is not recognized in his own place.'[4] Its choice for the Annunciation event appears strange, given the importance of Bethlehem as the place of Jesus' birth, Jerusalem as the climax of the story and the Sea of Galilee as the site of his ministry. Nazareth is not mentioned in the Old Testament. It was not included in the list of settlements of the tribes of Zebulun,[5] which mentions 12 towns and 6 villages. Nor was it included among the 45 cities of Galilee mentioned by the Jewish historian, Josephus;[6] and it is also missing from the 63 towns mentioned in the Talmud. But in spite of its disputed origins, Nazareth will always be honoured because the first Christians were called 'Nazarenes' (mentioned by Tertullian); and Jesus will always be called Jesus of Nazareth, not of Bethlehem.

But Nazareth's strategic position gave that place a certain importance even as far back as the civilizations of Babylon and Egypt. Both north and south of where the town stands there had been scenes of great battles, including that of Megiddo, whose name means 'a scene of many battles'. Nazareth is on the road to the Roman town of Sepphoris, which was constructed by Herod Antipas during the boyhood of Jesus: it is likely that Mary's husband, Joseph, obtained work here – there would have been a fever of building activity and many elaborate, extravagant buildings.

However, some modern scholars argue that Nazareth, not Bethlehem, may be the place where Jesus was born, while others argue that Nazareth did not even exist at that time. The critical question is *when* exactly, and at what stage in the Roman period, Nazareth came into existence; that is, whether settlement there began before or after 70 AD (the First Jewish War). The American archaeologist, James Strange, noted that Nazareth was not mentioned in ancient Jewish sources earlier than the third century AD, and assumed that this reflected its lack of prominence both in Galilee and in Judaea. Strange – supposing the existence of a settlement – originally guessed Nazareth's population at the time of Christ to be 'roughly 1,600 to 2,000 people', but later, 'a maximum of about 480'.[7] Yet there is definitely some evidence of settlement as far back as the Bronze and Iron ages.[8] Known as an all-Jewish, conservative town until the fourth century AD, Nazareth can be considered as a 'settler town' in what had become 'Galilee of the Gentiles'. These settlers would have been brought in from Judaea, and like all settlers, tended towards a conservative nationalism.

Some have argued that the absence of textual references to Nazareth in the Old Testament, the Talmud and Josephus, suggests that a town called 'Nazareth' did not exist at all in Jesus' day. Possibly it was only a small hamlet – this is how St Jerome described it in the fourth century.[9] The choice of Nazareth is clearly mysterious, but maybe St Jerome has the answer to the mystery. In his commentary on Isaiah, in particular on Isaiah 11.1 ('There shall come forth a shoot from the stump of Jesse, and a branch [Hebrew *netzer*] from his roots shall bear fruit'), Jerome writes:

> What all the churchmen seek and do not find in the prophets, that is, where it stands written: He will be called a Nazarene (Matt. 2.23), scholars of the Hebrews are of the opinion that it is taken from this passage (Isa. 11.1).[10]

So, writes Bargil Pixner (a Benedictine monk from Tabgha by the Sea of Galilee), the title Nazarene/Natzorean refers more to the Davidic descent of Jesus and not so much to his town of origin. Further, since excavations show that this small hamlet at the time of Jesus perhaps contained no more than 120–150 people, it is likely that it belonged to the larger village of Japhia nearby, a strongly fortified village that played a part in the war against the Romans (66–70 AD). And perhaps this clan, composed (supposedly) of the wider family group of Jesus, had come from Babylon around 100 BC, when a great immigration of Diaspora Jews from Persia and Babylon occurred.[11]

Moving to the present from the tiny hamlet of Jesus' day, Nazareth is now the largest Arab city in Israel. In fact, life in Nazareth is now a microcosm of what it is like to be Palestinian in Israel. Until the beginning of the British Mandate in Palestine (1922–48), its population was predominantly Arab Christian, the majority being Greek Orthodox, with an Arab Muslim minority. Nazareth today still has a significantly large Christian population, with flourishing congregations of Maronites, Greek Orthodox, Coptics among others. The Muslim population has grown for a number of historical factors. These include the city having served as an administrative centre under British rule, and the influx of Palestinian refugees absorbed into the city from neighbouring towns due to the dispossession of the villages (*al-Nakba* – 'the catastrophe', see page 11) in 1948. Its population is now almost exclusively Palestinian Arab, a quarter being internal refugees.[12]

To look out over the crowded town from the rooftops of the house of one of Nazareth's Christian families – with its own story of displacement from one of the Galilean villages – is to take in a snapshot of Nazareth's problems as well as those of Palestinians in Israel (of which there are 1.2 million, a minority in a Jewish State). Nazareth is closed, like a ghetto, with no open spaces, no green spaces, no industry (apart from tourism) and no future,[13] prohibited from expanding into the surrounding countryside. The majority of its people are poor, 137,330 families living below the poverty line. This means poor, overcrowded housing, high unemployment and poor health and a high infant mortality rate. Water problems are severe; there is much discrimination against Palestinians, though the situation is not as severe as in the West Bank. Thousands of 'illegal' homes have been built here – and elsewhere in Israel – and are under threat of demolition. According to the Jewish activist, Jeff Halper of ICAHD (Israeli Committee Against Housing Demolition), the conditions for acquiring a building permit are so difficult that Palestinians in desperation often build houses without permits, thus risking demolition.[14]

The challenge now is how to derive meaning and hope from Nazareth's past in the light of its present complexities: how can the event of Annunciation help us along the journey to peace?

Annunciation – then and now

With this historical background and present troubling situation, I revisit, in some awe, the figure of the young Jewish woman, Mary of Nazareth. She is the focus of the event at Nazareth that – as was mentioned earlier – inspired a Christian art tradition that is still vibrant. For Christians, Mary is the most revered woman in Scripture and has always occupied a special place in the hearts of Catholics. John Dear remarks, however, that as more attention has been given in recent years to women's spirituality and the Sacred Feminine, Mary is now also cherished by many Protestants.[15] And few Christians realize that Mary is also deeply venerated in Islam: with Hadija and Asiya, wives of the Prophet Muhammad, and Fatima, his daughter, she is one of the four women in whom Islamic tradition recognizes the 'station' of perfection. It is reported that when the Prophet was clearing the idols out of the Kaaba in Mecca, he allowed a fresco of the Virgin Mary holding the child Jesus to remain. In every mosque, the 'mihrab', or prayer niche, in the wall is dedicated to Mary. In the Qur'an, she is described as having been sent as 'a mercy for the worlds'.

'Mercy for the worlds' is the inspirational idea of Mary offered as a beginning of this reflection. Mercy is integral to the goal of reconciliation. Whereas Mary is revered most of all as mother of Jesus, as *theotokos* or God-bearer primarily in the Orthodox Churches, and has borne myriad titles and honours through the ages, it is as 'mercy for the worlds', as guide to the way of peace, that she is approached here.

Let us imagine her, first, in her historical context, about to become a mother in Israel and thus to play a crucial role in the redemption story. Like village mothers in Asia and Africa today, the lives of poor Jewish women were tough and exhausting, as they coped with the daily tasks of care for those in an extended, multi-generational family, agricultural work in the fields, olive groves (or in vegetable gardens/plots near the household), or mending fishing nets, baking bread and weaving clothes. We have very few studies of women's work in the New Testament – the issue is part of the invisibility and silence that surrounds women in the Scriptures.[16] There are also only relatively few examples of women's leadership or scholarship. Miriam, Esther and Deborah are examples of female leadership, and it is possible that Judith belonged to an ascetic sect and was steeped in learning. With the possible exception of Queen Esther, none of these were mothers. The wives of the patriarchs were valued because of the children they bore. Motherhood in the Hebrew Bible was often fraught with danger: the midwives Shiprah and Puah (Exod. 1) rescued the Hebrew babies from Pharaoh's murderous edict; the Holy Innocents were killed by Herod after the birth of Jesus.

Here a negative note demands attention: not only has devotion to Mary often been an ecumenical stumbling block, but also part of the reason why motherhood has been essentialized by tradition as the virtuous way to holiness for women, along with the alternative pathway of complete abstinence from sexual activity as consecrated virgins. The uniqueness of Mary lay in combining the two! Fortunately, rather than focusing on contested doctrines like the virginal conception and birth, recent theology has stimulated more enriching and historically accurate understandings of Mary. In Latin America, Maria Clara Bingemer and Yvone Gebara see her as Mother of the Poor, the prophetic Mary of the Magnificat who raises her voice in the name of all poor, cast-down women.[17] Rosemary Radford Ruether understands Mary as the first redeemed believer, thus a figure of the Church.[18] Hence she has a mothering role in an ecclesial symbolic sense. But this does not quite do justice to any role Mary has in redemption specifically as mother. In fact the bodily experience of Mary tends to be erased by an exclusively symbolic function. I think it is with Mary, if we can disentangle all unnecessary accretions of devotion around her, that we discover the practice of a profound spirituality of motherhood as integral to the practice of contemplation. The poem above tried to express this, as part of the creative mothering of God: 'O speak not a word, lest you miss what is born / From the womb of the Godhead creating with pain'.[19]

The Catholic Church has always stressed the importance of Mary's fiat in the Annunciation story, her obedient assent to God's word. But this has sometimes served to stress the passive obedience of women to their superiors, be they father, husband or son, and emphasized obedience as unflinching acceptance of authority, on whatever flawed basis this might rest.

The historical context for the Annunciation and the birth narratives is the Roman occupation of Palestine and what this meant for poor Jewish families. A recent study by Elizabeth Johnson, *Truly Our Sister*, helps to develop this historical perspective: she depicts Mary as a young Jewish girl, in the socio-geographical context of Galilee.[20] This means that we have to put aside the famous depictions of Mary from our Western traditions, beloved though they may be, of a beautifully dressed Mary, usually in white and blue, who, awaiting Gabriel's message, is discovered prayerfully reading a book. This is not the right place to discuss all the Marian dogmas. Mary as a poor peasant girl, with all the responsibilities just mentioned, is the focus. She was probably illiterate, given statistics for peasant communities then and knowing what we know now about the illiteracy of women globally in peasant communities. Yet she is a person of deep faith, schooled in Jewish Scriptures, through listening to synagogue prayer and the oral prayer tradition, in addition to her own life of prayer. She is a young woman, strengthened by this faith, capable of courage, action, and willing to make a risk-taking response to God. As Johnson writes: 'A woman of spirit, she embarks on the task of partnering God in the work of redemption.'[21]

Another possibility may shed light on the whole narrative, and even harmonize the stories of Matthew and Luke. We know from the Dead Sea Scrolls found at Qumran that it was possible at that time, even for a girl, to take a vow of chastity, of sexual abstinence as a way of consecration to God. Her father could nullify such a vow, if taken without his consent. Bargil Pixner thinks that Joseph, who was, according to tradition, older than Mary, could have been married before, was now a widower, and would already have a family (hence Jesus' half-brothers, frequently referred to by the Gospels): 'Mary's father could have trusted her to a man, who was prepared to acknowledge such a vow. Seeing that the widowed Joseph (of Davidic line), already had children, he could have found it easier to agree.'[22]

This idea transforms the character of Mary's response to Gabriel. It makes her willingness to cooperate with God's will even more amazing, as this request complicated her vow of consecrated virginity to God and would make the conception of Jesus yet more mysterious. Ultimately, the manner of Jesus' conception stresses, not an undervaluing of human sexuality, but God's initiative in grace. In addition, it opens up other spiritual paths for us today,[23] especially the Catholic intuition that virginal motherhood is the basis of Mary's spiritual charism. In and through her maternal role, Mary was faithful to contemplative meditation (Luke 2.51).

Through this lens it is possible to reinterpret many of the scriptural scenes that appear to give Mary a passive role. For example, the Marriage Feast of Cana in John's Gospel (John 2) indicates Mary's deep perceptive intuitiveness as to this being a *kairos* moment for Jesus' ministry. We are also able to move the perception of motherhood from its confinement to the domestic scene – something that in Western Europe dates only from the nineteenth century – to its wider social context. The responsible role given to mothers in the time of Mary, despite the patriarchal context and the poverty, contests the theory that women were always and everywhere oppressed. It could also be said of medieval Europe – even if this is a huge generalization – that despite the inferior position of women, if there was no desperate poverty and no war, there was a degree of respect for women as responsible for the intergenerational household. In a similar way, there was respect for Abbesses, who sometimes held responsibility for double monasteries and exercised the role of spiritual motherhood: I think of Hilda of Whitby, of Hildegard of Bingen, and of the wisdom of the anchoress Julian of Norwich, for whom *Jesus was our mother*.

This wider view of motherhood and Mary's spiritual charism does not take away from her own vulnerability: in the Advent journey we have undertaken, moving from conflict to reconciliation, she has become a symbol of hope for vulnerable, violated mothers and countless women raped in, for example, the recent genocides of Darfur (in the Sudan), the Balkans and Rwanda, the continuing gang-raping of women in the Democratic Republic of Congo, and domestic violence in our own countries. This symbolic role does not have to be based on Mary's actually having to undergo these experiences (although she experienced poverty under an occupation, fled Herod's violence as a refugee and kept on compassionately loving a son as his actions led to a brutal death), but on the part she has always played in the redeeming way her son would open to reconciliation. Gerard Manley Hopkins expressed this poignantly as a *present* reality:

> Of her flesh he took flesh:
> He does take fresh and fresh,
> Though much the mystery how,
> Not flesh but spirit now
> And makes, O marvellous!
> New Nazareths in us,
> Where she shall yet conceive
> Him morning, noon and eve;
> New Bethlems, and he born
> There, evening, noon and morn –
> Bethlem or Nazareth,
> Men here may draw like breath
> More Christ and baffle death[24]

Resisting violence against women: the inspiration of Mary

I want to call on Mary's prophetic inspiration, on her courage and openness to the Spirit specifically in the context of the current growing phenomenon of the trafficking of women and children. A recent report[25] of the UK-based Medaille community, which has committed itself to the wellbeing of trafficked women, estimates that:

> while it is impossible to know the full extent of trafficking, because of its underground nature, hundreds of thousands of women and children are sex-trafficked each year.[26]

Although a British Home Office Report estimated that 2,000 women and children are sex-trafficked into Britain each year, others say that figure is more realistically 10,000.[27] The trade is international, well organized, brutal, highly profitable – and growing. There are many causes: poverty, gender-based violence, gender discrimination within the family and the community, patriarchal models of the family, illiteracy, low levels of education, unemployment, lack of access to social services, single parenthood, sexual tourism, lack of information about the realities and dangers of trafficking, racism, xenophobia and discrimination, absence of legal immigration channels, breakdown of social and cultural values, and breakdown of communities. This formidable list is further fed by the involvement of transnational organized criminal networks, lack of both appropriate legislation and the political will to tackle trafficking.[28] The list has a formal and detached note, remote from the personal, anguished stories of thousands of women the world over. I have experienced some of these personally in India, where I saw the insoluble problems of women swept up into prostitution, and their apparent inability to change their situations. The desperation in their faces, a mixture of shame and hopelessness, was only relieved by their hopes for their children: that their little girls should not be swept into the same trade, and should have a different future, gave them a reason for living.

The horror of this situation seems far away from the Angelic Annunciation to Mary of Nazareth; and yet not so far from modern-day Nazareth. A teacher attending the seventh Sabeel International Conference in Nazareth in 2008 revealed to participants that many of the mothers of the schoolchildren she taught were forced, through poverty, into prostitution. Mary herself, immediately after the birth of her child, would become a refugee, and her son, as part of his ministry, would directly confront women trapped in these degrading situations. Prostitution and trafficking were all too real threats for women, then as now. The violence of military conflict, the deception surrounding torture regimes, the glossing over of sexual crimes of soldiers on all sides of the wars or the blatantly open provision of 'comfort women' to soldiers – these are realities that pose challenges for all on a journey to peace with justice. So how does Mary's encounter with the Holy Spirit in Nazareth offer any hope to us now?

The Holy Spirit – the 'Go-Between God'

In 1972, a former Bishop of Winchester, John Taylor, wrote a book called *The Go-Between God*.[29] In it, in an inspirational way, he developed a theology of the Holy Spirit as the energy – or force field – drawing people together in relation. He used the word *annunciation* to express the relational encounter of mutuality – inspired by the New Testament Annunciation story. This beautifully encapsulates Mary's receptivity and openness, despite her fear and bewilderment at what is being asked. The depth of encounter with the Spirit is expressive both of the life of consecrated commitment that I am suggesting was her choice, as well as of the spirituality of contemplation she offers us. Annunciations – or *epiphanies of connection* as I call them (see the Epilogue to this book), as this better captures the idea of mutual encounter – evoke the experience of an encounter that transcends known possibilities, reaching out into the mystery of otherness and difference that challenges anyone on the path to reconciliation. The encounter begins in the prayer of stillness: the prayer of rapt attention draws Mary into a depth of communion. It was John Taylor, in his many poetic examples of the annunciation idea, who first drew me to the Jewish thinker, Martin Buber, as inspiration for 'I–Thou' mutuality, an important concept in peacemaking processes. Buber traced the source for the I–Thou to the very beginnings of Creation: his insistence on 'In the beginning was the Relation' stressed God's longing for relation as the reason for the world's coming into being. The American feminist theologian, Carter Heyward, has developed this leitmotif in her groundbreaking 1982 book, *The Redemption of God*.[30] In the last 25 years there has been a great cloud of witnesses as to the empowering dynamics of relational theology, both in feminist theology and beyond. Many who tread this path have experienced that the ideas of mutuality, connection, compassion, wisdom, relation and relational justice have continued to inspire and sustain all on the spiritual journey, especially the journey from conflict to reconciliation. At the heart of this theology is the notion that God is our passion for justice, inspiring the journey at every point. Justice is at the heart of faith because our concern for justice is fuelled by God's very self. It is not an optional add-on. Philip

Newell of the Iona Community saw justice as the very heartbeat of God.[31]

In the beginning was God. In the beginning was relation, because God is the power and energy of our relating and yearning for justice and right relation. Whether we speak about God's creation, God's embodying in Jesus to heal the broken connections, or the flame of the Spirit at Pentecost, birthing communities of connection, we are speaking of God's passion for justice, for healed relationships among all people, and creatures. If the divine purpose for creation is the remaking of broken connections or reconciliation, justice and peace are the way to achieving this. Our passion for justice confronts the fact that though we yearn for mutual relation, broken relation is in fact what surrounds, even overwhelms us, on personal, community and international levels.

'Annunciation' is iconic in showing how Mary is integral to this passion for relational justice. If Jesus became the embodiment of mutuality-in-relation, then it was from his mother that he first learnt this spirituality. Mary's creative encounter with the Holy Spirit points the way to the healing of broken relation. *This is her gift to us for the Advent journey*. The force field of mutuality may seem light years away from the brutality of rape, torture, Jewish memories of the Holocaust and the daily humiliations of Palestinians at the Israeli checkpoints. It is a gift because, first, as the famous icon of the Virgin and child, the *Hodogetria*,[32] tells us, she is pointing towards Christ, the child of reconciliation. As Rowan Williams explains:

> For our hands to point towards Jesus, we have to have been sufficiently moved out of our usual ways of thought and action to want to say, 'Don't look at me, look at him.' . . . When I encounter . . . failure in my experience, I am challenged deeply about my habitual longing to be in control and at the centre; I have to move out from the centre that is my self-image and, in my action, in my body, *mark out a path towards truth*.[33]

Whereas in Chapter 1, through John the Baptist, the pilgrim is called to repent, and in our own times to turn to the earth so as to live in harmony with her rhythms, the Annunciation encounter of Mary and the Spirit invite us to take a second step, namely to practise a spirituality of contemplation, turning towards the child of reconciliation.

It is the path towards truth, mentioned above and in Chapter 1. Resting in the force field of mutuality, in the longing for the healing of broken relation, the ability emerges of paying attention to the full horror of what is blocking peace and allowing the brutal systems of trafficking of women and children. The point is not to deny the horror, or let it deceive us.

I suggest that this 'paying attention' that is at the heart of a spirituality of contemplation paves the way for changed consciousness. The Thomas Merton Association of Great Britain called their 2010 conference 'Awakening the Paradise Mind', remembering that Merton devoted his whole life to the practice of contemplation to restore this consciousness: 'Here is an unspeakable secret: paradise is all around us and we do not understand. It is wide open . . . "Wisdom", cries the dawn deacon, but we do not attend.'[34]

Changed consciousness moulded Merton into becoming a passionate prophet of peace, still inspirational today. *Paying attention* as contemplative practice in ever-widening circles has a long genealogy, from the French spiritual writer and activist, Simone Weil, through the novelist-philosopher Iris Murdoch, to the contemporary ecofeminist theologian, Sallie McFague. For Simone Weil, it was a form of 'waiting on God', sustaining attentiveness to God's will that became a lifelong stance for her.[35] Sallie McFague developed a similar contemplative practice of 'seeing with the loving eye' as an invitation to relate to nature that is different from 'seeing with the dominant eye', the eye that wishes to control, leading to destructive policies towards the earth.[36] These are all different ways of describing the attempt to recover what is called in Catholic tradition the sacramental way of beholding reality, of experiencing creation filled with the presence of God, and in spirituality the reverencing of the ordinary daily living.

Rowan Williams has developed this in a recent book, *Dostoevsky: Language, Faith and Fiction*, writing of the moment of revelation that can be disclosed from *paying attention to ordinary things*:[37]

> By taking the step of loving attention in the mundane requirements of life together, something is *disclosed*. But that step is itself enabled by a prior disclosure, the presence of gratuity in and behind the phenomena of the world: of some unconditional love.

This is surely what John Taylor meant by *annunciations*, and recalls the profundity of Mary's praying attentiveness as a stance of daily living. That it also may evoke a sense of transfiguration, of moving beyond normal boundaries, is poignantly described by the Benedictine, Mark Hederman, in his encounter with Iris Murdoch in the last difficult period of her life as she suffered from Alzheimer's disease.[38] In his book, *Walkabout: Life as Holy Spirit,* Hederman, now Abbot of Glenstal Abbey in Limerick, describes his spiritual journey that is sensitive to the promptings of the Holy Spirit. He develops a theology of Spirit open to beauty, art, literature, to time, place and synchronicity. At this period he was attentive to the Spirit's invitations in many ways. All his life he had been influenced by Iris Murdoch, finding that a particular novel she had written spoke to the moment of his own quest. Her last novel, *Jackson's Dilemma,*[39] was written when she was already descending into Alzheimer's, but witnesses to the power of the Spirit at an unconscious level. Jackson, Hederman writes, 'is the Holy Spirit, son of "This Jack, joke, poor potsherd, patch, matchwood" that ultimately "Is immortal diamond".'[40]

Mark Hederman felt increasingly that he must meet with Iris Murdoch before her death, to tell her how much her work spoke to him. Eventually a meeting came to pass at her home in Oxford, and this is how her husband, John Bayley, recorded their conversation:

> ... when the tall monk and Iris sat down together, things changed at once. They became extraordinarily animated – she starting sentences, or ending them – he appearing to know at once what she wanted to ask, and filling the words they were failing to make with a professional abundance of loving kindness. And yet his face looked really transfigured: so, a few moments later, did hers. They were soon on about his childhood, why he joined the order, most of all about his plans to make discussion of her works a regular thing at Glenstal Abbey.[41]

John Bayley described this meeting between the monk and the novelist as an epiphany, very much in the sense of what Taylor meant by 'annunciation'. Here, it is this sense of being transfigured, becoming open to the transcendent, communicating below the surface that is significant for our journey to peace. Hederman believed that Iris Murdoch, in her inner monastery, was in communion with God. Rowan Williams's reaction to the icon of Virgin and child, the

Hodogetria, raised the issue of self-knowledge and moved the focus of attention away from the selfish ego to discover a God-oriented centre, the movement from the false to the true self.

This is the moment to make the connections with the violence of our times, the horrific situations of trafficking and rape just cited. When these realities appear too overwhelming to face:

> Mary teaches us that the first step on the road to peace is to become people of contemplative nonviolence. That means, like Mary, we need to sit in solitude and listen for God. It means giving God our violence, brokenness, anger, pain, bitterness, resentments, helplessness, and powerlessness. It means allowing God to disarm our hearts, give us the gift of peace, and send us forth into the war-making world on a peace-making mission.[42]

Far from renouncing activism, legal reform or personal responsibility for the victims of violence (all essential), the stance of contemplation directs our focus on this Advent journey from the murderers, the perpetrators of genocide and military brutality, to our own responsibility for violence and lack of justice. On this pilgrimage towards Christmas, none of us are the great innocents. We are all caught up in the confrontational mentality of our age and have areas of unreconciled issues in our families and personal relationships. We find it impossible, from one side of a conflict, to 'see with the eyes of another', to enter and inhabit the truth of another with empathy and understanding. So family feuds are passed from generation to generation. This is exactly where the Holy Spirit's Annunciation encounters move us forward into seeking a reconciling truth. Taylor's book is redolent with stories of the I–Thou force field of the Spirit leading people into exactly this empathic understanding that can lead to reconciliation and forgiveness.

The stance of contemplative attention ushers in this possibility, beginning with ourselves and the sense of being locked into guilt, remorse or helplessness, as we realize our complicity in the world's cruel systems. We are called to pay attention to our own truth, to become increasingly aware, as we dwell within our inner monasteries, of the historical role we have played in different conflicts and how, rather than lapse into bitterness and despair, another way forward is at hand. The final stage is in moving from contemplation to action: the Holy Spirit never leaves us immobilized but, like Mary, empowered into action for peacemaking.

From contemplation to action

She is rushing through hillside, her sister she seeks,
In the mutual joy of encounter she speaks:
'God is listening, hearing, all history's sorrow,
God is with me, creating, and birthing tomorrow . . .'[43]

As Chapter 1 related,[44] Mary lost no time in journeying over the hills from Nazareth to the home of Elizabeth at Ein Kerem. Taylor's Annunciation is written in the context of mission, of sending. Mary has moved from stillness to action and then to the prophetic action for non-violent peacemaking. The next step of our journey is to follow her to Bethlehem.

Fast forward: Nazareth – the beginning of Jesus' mission

But before we take the road to Bethlehem, we take a minute to look to the future, to the event believed to be the beginning of Jesus' ministry, in the synagogue of Nazareth, now a Christian church, beautiful in its simplicity.

Into the synagogue of his home town of Nazareth enters the young Rabbi Jesus, and the level of expectancy of the local people, presumably including neighbours and family, is high. He is given the scroll and it falls open at the reading for the day, Isaiah 61.1–7:

'The Spirit of the Lord is upon me, because he has anointed me to proclaim good news to the poor. He has sent me to proclaim liberty to the captives and recovering of sight to the blind, to set at liberty those who are oppressed, to proclaim the year of the Lord's favour.'[45]

But did it actually fall open here, or did Luke choose this text as the solemn proclamation inaugurating Jesus' ministry? Luke could never have envisaged the impact this text would have through the ages, even inspiring a new revolutionary order. James Massey, in his Dalit Bible commentary, sees the 'Nazareth Manifesto' as Jesus reaching out to the most oppressed, outcastes and outsiders, in his case referring specifically to the Dalit communities.[46] Whether or not Jesus or Luke intended the passage to have such a revolutionary meaning, for this journey to peace and reconciliation, what is crucial is to keep in mind the dynamic connection between Gabriel's greeting and its whole-hearted acceptance by Mary of Nazareth. It was this that drove her to embark on her own journey, first across the Judaean hills, then taking the road to Bethlehem. Unaware how the future would unfold, her actions enable this coming child to take upon himself the world's need for reconciliation, and begin to enunciate the vast scope of this peacemaking mission to a hostile crowd in Nazareth. But before this happened, *the message of peace will be proclaimed at Bethlehem.*

3

The Nativity

Oh broken town of Bethlehem
Your people long for peace,
But curfews, raids and closure barricades
Have brought them to their knees.
Yet still they strive for justice
And still they make their stand
Their hopes and fears still echo down the years
Come, heal this holy land.[1]

But you, O Bethlehem of Ephrathah, who are one of the little clans of
Judah, from you shall come forth for me one who is to rule in Israel.

(Mic. 5.2)

The reality that is Bethlehem today

Bethlehem, House of Bread (Hebrew), House of Meat (Arabic), now
becomes the focus of this Advent–Christmas journey to peace, for the
simple reason that Christian tradition claims that Jesus was born
here.[2] Bethlehem is one of the most treasured destinations of Christian
pilgrimages – along with the Church of the Holy Sepulchre in
Jerusalem. Yet if a person were now to stand in Manger Square (the
centre of the old town), watching the many pilgrimage coaches roll
in from numerous countries, she/he would see that the average time
spent in the town would be around 30 minutes: enough time to visit
the Church of the Nativity and the many gift shops – a major part
of Bethlehem's economy – and possibly the Peace Centre, built in
2000. Then it will be on to Shepherds' Field and Jericho. But the
reality of what it means to be a Bethlehemite today will remain
hidden. On my first visit in 2006, attending lectures at Bethlehem

University for the sixth Sabeel International Conference, even glimps-
ing the Church of the Nativity proved not to be possible as there had
been an unexpected incursion of 40 Israeli tanks into Bethlehem, near
Manger Square. These had surrounded an area and started to destroy
a house that was home to six or eight families. Israeli soldiers shot
dead two young men from the Hassan and Obayat families – the
Obayat family are possibly descendants of the biblical shepherds – and
injured a few more, including an elderly woman of 86 who is now
brain damaged. Anger and grief filled the town. Out of respect, we
were asked not to visit the area. This gives some idea of how the
traditional birthplace of Jesus is today 'one of the most contentious
places on earth', as Michael Finkel wrote in a controversial late-2007
article in the *National Geographic* magazine:

> This is not how Mary and Joseph came into Bethlehem, but this is how
> you enter now. You wait at the Wall. It's a daunting concrete barricade,
> three stories high, thorned with razor wire. Standing beside it, you feel
> as if you're at the base of a dam. Israeli soldiers armed with assault rifles
> examine your papers. They search your vehicle. No Israeli civilian, by
> military order, is allowed in. And few Bethlehem residents are permitted
> out – the reason the wall exists here, according to the Israeli government,
> is to keep terrorists away from Jerusalem.
>
> Bethlehem and Jerusalem are only six miles apart (ten kilometers),
> though in the compressed and fractious geography of the region, this
> places them in different realms. It can take a month for a postcard to
> go from one city to the other. Bethlehem is in the West Bank, on land
> taken by Israel during the Six Day War of 1967. It's a Palestinian city; the
> majority of its 35,000 residents are Muslim. In 1900, more than 90 percent
> of the city was Christian. Today Bethlehem is only about one-third
> Christian, and this proportion is steadily shrinking as Christians leave
> for Europe or the Americas. At least a dozen suicide bombers have come
> from the city and surrounding district. The truth is that Bethlehem, the
> 'little town' venerated during Christmas, is one of the most contentious
> places on earth.
>
> If you're cleared to enter, a sliding steel door, like that on a boxcar,
> grinds open. The soldiers step aside, and you drive through the temporary
> gap in the wall. Then the door slides back, squealing on its track, boom-
> ing shut. You're in Bethlehem.[3]

Finkel's graphic picture is a dramatic but somewhat distorted representation of a complex reality. Some aspects of the reality missed by so many tourists are offered, and some useful information given; unfortunately, however, he propagates the one-sided stereotyping that often mars such accounts, namely that Palestinians in Bethlehem are 'radical', feared by Israelis and so on. Like seething water, they must be contained. The fact that it takes a month for a letter to reach Jerusalem, far from being due to a non-functioning postal system, is because of the enforced isolation of Bethlehem.

Since the election victory of Hamas[4] in Gaza, this stereotyping has worsened. Finkel also gives the impression that there are insoluble tensions between Christians and Muslims and that this is the reason for the large Christian emigration from the West Bank and Gaza. But there are many other rich layers to Palestinian life and culture that go unmentioned and will be explored here. The truth is that Christians and Muslims have lived together here – and elsewhere – harmoniously for centuries.[5]

But the fundamental reality his account successfully opens up is that this most sacred place for Christians (important for all three Abrahamic faiths), housing 22 Christian churches and 11 mosques, is now in reality a great prison in the West Bank. To begin with, the historic entrance road to Bethlehem, where Joseph and Mary would have travelled, used to pass by Rachel's tomb, a holy site for both Jews and Christians. This is now blocked off for the Christians of Bethlehem by the great separation Wall, the 'daunting concrete barricade' referred to by Finkel: the Wall, planned to be 700 km long, is officially intended for Israeli 'security'. (Many argue that this is less a 'security' wall than a demarcation of expanding Israeli territory.) The Wall now encircles the old cities of Bethlehem and Beit Jala to the west of Bethlehem, and the northern part of Beit Sahour (the original site of the Shepherds' Field). Thus access to the ancient pathway is cut off, and effectively only two entrances are allowed. The Israelis control who will be allowed in and out. Some of the families suffering the effects of the path of this huge Wall were present at the Sabeel conference in 2006 I referred to above. Khalid is cut off from his grocery shop, and therefore his livelihood. Claire Anastas's family has lost their business, and the Wall now dominates the view from every room. Both her parents have died as a result of the trauma they have undergone.[6] 'We are imprisoned in a tomb', she has frequently said. Yet despite such traumas, bereavements, economic collapse and daily harassments, the Wall continues to expand, to snake its inexorable progress into Palestinian territory.

The effect on business and economic life in general has been devastating, as acres of olive groves, vineyards, precious fruit trees and agricultural land lie on the other side of the Wall and Palestinian farmers have no right of access to their own land. Families have become separated. To add to the constrictions, a whole set of new roads accessible only to Israelis have been built, clearly visible from Bethlehem. People are forced to find circuitous alternative routes. Out of 80 businesses, 72 have closed along the Jerusalem road. Between 17,000 and 18,000 people still live in the refugee camps – Bethlehem has three of these. Michael Finkel depicts them as:

> boxy apartments heaped atop one another in haphazard piles. Every breeze through the camp' alleys ruffles the corners of hundreds of martyrs' posters – young men, staring impassively, some gripping M-16s. Many are victims of the Israel Defense Forces. Others have blown themselves up in an Israeli mall or restaurant or bus. Arabic text on the posters extols the greatness of these deeds.[7]

Again, Finkel's description captures one aspect of a complex reality. He describes posters, not human beings, and gives no sense of daily life being carried on. His descriptions of militant Palestinians conveniently ignore the ever-present border guards in Bethlehem and the weekly – even daily – incursions of the Israelis into the camps. However, as part of our journey many other hopeful features of these camps and the daily living of a people with haunted memories of lost villages will be described here.

Bethlehem revisited

In my next visit to Israel and Palestine, in 2008, I stayed at Tantur Ecumenical Institute, situated on a hill looking towards Bethlehem and the broad hills that surround it. Unlike in the days of Luke and of Jesus, these once bare hills are now covered with illegal Israeli settlements. Their gradual encroachment on Palestinian land is threatening the very existence and survival of the Palestinian people. In Bethlehem district there are 27 Israeli settlements and 73,000 settlers on Bethlehem's land. The huge settlement of Har Homa towers over the old city. Har Homa – once a beautiful forested hill – plans to develop an alternative Israeli-controlled tourist industry for Bethlehem, further threatening the fragile Palestinian economy. To travel along the Jerusalem–Jericho road today is a grim experience: the reality of the encroachment of the settlements becomes very clear. The beginning is an innocuous looking observation tower at the top of a hill. This then expands eventually into the huge settlements to be seen on every horizon, and I saw no hill without a watchtower. At the time of writing, the issue of settlements is blocking even the possibility of peace talks taking place between Israelis and Palestinians.[8]

Many Bedouin 'encampments' can be seen along this road. These are poor tin shacks, where people and animals are crowded. Because the Bedouin people have lost their land, they can no longer be nomadic. The evictions of 1948 and seizure of land (described in Chapter 1) meant that Bedouin lifestyle underwent a radical transformation. For example, the goat-hair tent has become a dwelling consisting of poor metal shelters constructed using old water containers. Overcrowded camps have become the norm, where people and animals share a very limited space that has no running water, sewage system or electricity.[9] An enforced sedentary life style has meant that the Bedouins now suffer from illnesses previously unknown to them, such as diabetes. And everywhere the Wall cuts off access to their land, to other people, as well as to Jerusalem.[10]

Checkpoints control entry and exit to and from Bethlehem, and permits are not easy to obtain. In fact the selective and restrictive distribution of permits is the essence of the occupational control system. The Wall is visible; the oppressive nature of the permit system is not. It can mean that people are afraid to engage in non-violent acts of protest for fear they will be refused permission to visit their loved ones. Many families are now separated. Nor are the checkpoints predictable: 'flying checkpoints' appear without notice. Harassment of the people is an increasing reality. At one point in our journey in 2006, at a checkpoint where a Palestinian Christian was discovered on our coach, we were forbidden access and had to make a long detour to find a checkpoint that would let us through. This happens all the time. An old checkpoint – Qalandia – outside Jerusalem has now been transformed to act as a large terminal and a border control. But the vast majority of checkpoints have nothing to do with borders: they are separating and harassing Palestinians in their own land, the 22 per cent of Palestine that they may still inhabit.

Toine van Teeffelen, a Bethlehem-based anthropologist and Development Educational director of the Arab Education Institute (AEI), writes of the deliberate dehumanization of Palestinians through this harassment:

> One of the most effective elements of occupation is the denial of Palestinians to think, feel and act like human beings with stories to act and tell. Much of the repression is to keep Palestinians in routine, predictable scripts, of submission and incidentally violent acts.[11]

The Israeli occupational discourse and actions on Palestinians regard them as objects of causal 'management' mechanisms. Much physical infrastructure, including checkpoints and the Wall structures, are physical metaphors and directed at 'pushing' Palestinians into daily inhuman routines/scripts (for example, corridors at checkpoints that are reminiscent of cattle structures). The Israeli discourse and actions about Gaza also take on a 'scientific experimental' mode: how far can you go with 'pressuring' a population into obedience?[12]

Every day, from the vantage point of Tantur, I looked out towards the Bethlehem checkpoint and saw the malevolent reality of the Wall. I saw the weary resigned faces of Palestinians passing through the checkpoint on their way home, steeling themselves for inevitable harassment. (They may even be ordered to strip.) I could almost hear the careless laughter of the young Israeli soldiers – both female and male – who staff this checkpoint, and smell their cigarette smoke. I could also glimpse in the morning mist the Mosque of Caliph Omar, who captured the Holy Places non-violently in 637 AD,[13] and hear the call to prayer, a dramatic reminder that this city is a pilgrim place for three faiths, embodying sites of great significance. I wondered if the Wall's route had been planned here around Bethlehem also because of the very sacredness of these sites.

Now, mindful of present realities, our journey tries to cross back over 2,000 years to the period when Luke was writing about this very city,[14] but with a specific purpose: by following his account of the special birth of this child of reconciliation, could sources of hope be uncovered not only for the peoples of the Bible lands, but for all in search of peace? Could our celebration of Christmas become transformed this year because of this?

Like the Palestinian people today, poor Jewish communities of the first century struggled not only to survive, but also to sustain lives of dignity. The Gospel writers clearly knew more stories about Jesus than they were able to tell us, so it is possible that Luke's text might disclose more if we ask different questions of it. Even if Luke had not visited Bethlehem, he spoke to eyewitnesses, including, it is supposed, to Mary, Jesus' mother.[15] We do not know what songs the people of Bethlehem sang, the poems they loved, what dances they danced when celebrating weddings and other festivals. It has been very difficult for feminist biblical scholars over the past 20 years to tease out the voices and stories of women rendered invisible and silenced by the text (and society). Is it possible that by looking and learning from contemporary Middle-Eastern culture, memories and scholarship, we might arrive at a more multi-layered understanding of the text that might also liberate narratives of hope and peace? For as Toine van Teeffelen wrote, citing the late, much mourned Edward Said:

> *Palestine suffers from story-crowdedness*, combining stories of the Holy Land, the Bible, East–West, pioneering missionaries, a place of rescue and homeland for Jews, and so on. This story density makes it particularly difficult for Palestinians to find their own voice. Their stories tend to become appropriated for other purposes, or are treated as expressions of underlying properties (threatening, emotional, voices as predictable scripts) and therefore are not listened to. It's a challenge to develop genres/platforms/practices of communication which help to reconnect and in which the word remains alive, does not become appropriated, or frozen.[16]

Can Gospel texts become sources of reconciliation and peace for the Advent journey today, offering hope for a conflict-ridden world?

Along the road to Bethlehem with Mary and Joseph

For Luke, the Christmas narrative was important for understanding the significance of Jesus. For the journey today, Luke is a theologian of peace and justice – his whole Gospel can be considered as a journey, even as a retelling of the Exodus story to freedom. The Advent journey today seeks reconciliation, and sees the Christmas story as inspiring its dynamic.

For Luke, though his historical and geographical knowledge is often faulty, a sense of history and context was important – but he is not primarily writing a history. He is in dialogue with a person, Theophilus, who is probably educated and wealthy. And he wants him to know the truth (1.4). So he gives a frame for the birth of Jesus through the story of another special birth, that of John. The first framing of Jesus' birth ends with the famous Magnificat (1.46–55), a prayer that continues to inspire hope in places of affliction and oppression. The next stage is ushered in by the birth of John (1.57–66). As we have seen, his father Zechariah's famous prayer, the Benedictus, is important in making it crystal clear that John will be a prophet: through this figure, Luke has introduced the themes that will frame his theology, namely prophecy, justice for those 'in darkness' and a pedagogy of peace.

No room at the inn?

The stories surrounding Jesus' birth are beloved of Christian tradition. At a popular level they are enshrined in the nativity plays of primary schools, children's Christmas services and numerous carols depicting the Christchild born in a cave on the hillside. Churches solemnize the season with dignity – for example, the Festival of Nine Lessons and Carols at King's College, Cambridge[17] – and exhort congregations not to fall prey to extravagant consumerism.

This is backed up by zealous efforts of charities to fundraise at Christmas by imagining the Holy Family as poverty-stricken, homeless and refugees. Given the weight of tradition, is it possible to orient the Advent preparation more towards peace, and to see the inspiration for this at the heart of the Gospels?

To begin with the 'born in a cave/stable tradition', there are numerous caves in and around Bethlehem, and the 'birth in a cave' tradition is a very early one. St Jerome travelled to Bethlehem and, according to tradition, translated the Bible in a cave adjoining what is now the Church of the Nativity. The apocryphal *Protoevangelion of Saint James* depicts a birth in a cave on the way to Bethlehem.[18] It is this document, in fact resembling a novel, on which the cave tradition was first based. Yet this writer knew nothing of the geography of Palestine and not much about Jewish tradition and culture. Justin Martyr, at the end of the first century, speaks of two shrines: one where Jesus was born and the manger in the cave in which he was laid. No one disputes the piety that grew up around the birth in a cave. Kenneth Bailey – who opens up for us important Arabic Christian traditions – cites the twentieth-century Coptic Orthodox scholar and monk, Father Matta al-Miskin, who reflects on Mary alone in the cave:

> My heart goes out to this solitary mother.
> How did she endure labor pains alone?
> How did she receive the child with her own hands?
> How did she wrap him while her strength was totally exhausted?
> What did she have to eat or drink?[19]

The truth could in fact be less romantic and more profound. Mothers around the world know that there is time to prepare for a birth even if you have to go on a journey you might not have chosen. Mary and Joseph would have been aware of the special nature of this baby, and the meaning of this event. Bailey suggests that as a member of the House of David, Joseph could have counted on hospitality with his kinsfolk in Bethlehem. These houses of the first century would have comprised a family room/living room, a room for the animals slightly lower down and a guest room on the other side or above (Elijah was offered a similar room by the widow of Zarephath; 1 Kings 17). The host family would have welcomed the couple, and the women would have assisted Mary with the birth of her baby – as women did the world over, before birth became medicalized and hospitalized. It would have been easy to reach into the animals' quarters for a manger, fill it with fresh straw, wrap the baby in the blanket and let him rest there. Another type of house is suggested by Toine van Teeffelen:

> Many Bethlehemites think that the Holy Family may have stayed in a house on top of a half-cave used for storing goods and keeping house animals. Such a cave was warm, private and therefore suitable for giving birth. The baby was afterwards laid in the manger normally used by the animals.[20]

The reason for the positive interpretation of the cave is, as Bailey thought, that Palestinians are hospitable people: they would never have turned the family away. It is also true that not only in Palestine but in many parts of the world, it is perfectly possible to live comfortably in a cave. Troglodytes have their own methods of adapting! But there is also a negative cave tradition: Mounir Fasheh, former director of the Palestinian 'Tamer' Institute for Community Education, said that:

> the fact that Christ was born in a cave, in a manger, is not a call to idolize or glorify the cave or the manger but a reminder to us of the absurd and evil conditions in the world. It is a call to action so that babies will not have to be born in a cold and unhealthy cave. Christ being born in a cave might seem exotic to Western tourists, but for us Palestinians, it is a reminder that the inhuman conditions under which Christ was born (including his flee[ing] with his parents to avoid being killed by soldiers) do still exist in the world and, in particular, in the very place where Christ was born.[21]

Both interpretations are opposed to a romanticized wilderness image of the cave as in the traditional Western depictions. Perhaps they also show the development of a theology focusing almost exclusively on dividing people into oppressors and victims, inflicting suffering or passively enduring it, to a more nuanced stage that is focused on here: more dimensions are taken into account, including the ability of people to move on with courage, cope with daily life with dignity, with pride in cultural values, sharing their lives with others, with a generous openness to guests. It evokes the possibility of a readiness to forgive, wherever there is a breakthrough from the consciousness of the dominant power. Given the oppressive context of the Wall/checkpoints/permits, does not the recovery of Jesus' birth story in the house of a poor family of Bethlehem, not in the commercialized space of the inn, not only symbolize the fragility of birth, but also the ability to create dignity in this shared, homely space? Even to experience a different sense of time? If so, how did we arrive at the wicked innkeeper who refused admittance, the familiar villain of the Christmas play? A possible solution is in the word used for 'inn' – Greek *kataluma* – which is not the same word used for the more commercial inn where the Good Samaritan left the wounded man along the Jericho road (Luke 15). *Kataluma* also means 'guest room'. So the family offered hospitality in their own living room, because their guest room – because of the census? – was already occupied. This does not quite explain the significance of the manger, but that is still to come.[22]

Shepherds on the hillside

This is the climax to the Lukan birth story (the way the visit of the Wise Men is for Matthew's Gospel). There are still sheep on the Bethlehem hillsides, and the reality of shepherding is still harsh, now for different reasons and mostly because of harassment from settlers and Israeli soldiers. Shepherds in biblical times were close to the lowest rung of society, widely regarded as unclean and dishonest – strange to our ears when the shepherd image is still revered as iconic of Christ, the Good Shepherd. Bailey suggests that this may be because flocks eat private property and that shepherds are included in lists of proscribed trades. Joachim Jeremias suggests that as herdsmen they led their flocks to other people's lands, and because of their thieving it was forbidden to buy wool, milk or kids from them.[23] No wonder they were poor! The idea of the lowliness of shepherds is well depicted in W. H. Auden's 'At the Manger', part of his Christmas Oratorio, *For the Time Being*. Here they express how the birth of Jesus has transformed their lives:

> THIRD SHEPHERD
> To-night for the first time the prison gates
> Have opened.
>
> FIRST SHEPHERD
> Music and sudden light

SECOND SHEPHERD
Have interrupted our routine tonight,
THIRD SHEPHERD
And swept the filth of habit from our hearts.
THE THREE SHEPHERDS
O here and now our endless journey starts.[24]

The poverty of the shepherds (Auden speaks of the 'solitude familiar to the poor'[25]), like the reality of the 'no room at the inn', again dispels any form of romanticism. In rural India, sheep and goats are still the only animals that poor people can afford. Even in times of famine and drought, the relief for animals tends to be focused on cattle, so there is more sickness and death among sheep and goats. So for Luke, it is immensely important that the message of the angels is heard as good news by the very poorest people. And these are shepherds near Bethlehem, the city of David – David who was himself once a shepherd. As they hurry to Bethlehem, the fact that the baby is in a poor person's house, and the child has been laid to rest in a manger, exactly where they would have placed their own newborn babies, is part of this good news. That they are received with honour is again traditional to Middle-Eastern hospitality, Bailey stresses.[26] It must surely be part of the reason they returned, 'glorifying and praising God'. And the message they gave to the world – they, the first witnesses of the birth – was one of 'on earth peace among those with whom he is pleased!' (Luke 2.14). That the *angels* proclaim peace is surely symbolic that heaven and earth are united in this wondrous event, as would be expressed by Jesus' own prayer, the 'Our Father':

> May your will be done,
> On earth as it is in heaven.[27]

This message of peace is at the heart of Luke's theology of peace and reconciliation, his constant theme as Jesus' life unfolds. Possibly he was influenced by the hopes of Augustus Caesar (whom he has already mentioned in citing the census[28]), and is hinting at the *Pax Augusta* alluded to in Virgil's Fourth Eclogue: 'Begin, little boy, to greet your mother with a smile.'[29]

But although some have claimed Virgil as a 'Christian before Christ', I draw a veil of caution over this, as what Luke means by peace is worlds away from what either Virgil or Augustus Caesar meant! Ultimately, as we shall see, it is a peace given through Christ's Resurrection, but its fruits of joy and healing are here even at the birth of this wondrous child. And behind the Christmas angels' words are again the words of Isaiah (9.3–6), especially in expressing the joy at the birth of 'Wonderful Counsellor, Mighty God, Everlasting Father, Prince of Peace' (Isa. 9.6).[30]

Of course the memory of the shepherds is still a vibrant part of the life of Bethlehem today: only 1,100 yards from the Church of the Nativity is the village of Beit Sahour, Village of the Watching, part of which the Wall encircles, as was mentioned earlier:

> There is a ruined field here known in Arabic as Deir (monastery) or Kanisat al-Ru'at (Church of the Shepherds). The underground church belonging to the Greek Orthodox is used here still on Sundays and at Christmas, and, until quite recent times, the Latins came here at 3 a.m. on Christmas morning. The Franciscan church 1100 yards away was not built until 1954, when a notice was placed there in Italian: Campo del Pastori (Shepherds' Field). A Byzantine monastery and church have been excavated here.[31]

But it is about much more than remembering the ancient shrine. The shepherds' cave tradition still flourishes in the caves around Bethlehem. Bedouin shepherds – alluded to earlier – are now forced to be poor, not because of Jewish tradition, but in many cases because of the evictions in 1948 and consequent loss of land, access to water and adequate fodder for animals.[32]

It is possible, writes Delia Khano, that the descendants of the biblical shepherds are the Ta'amreh – semi-Bedouins east of Bethlehem:

> The Ta'amreh are a Bedouin tribe who live near Bethlehem; they like to consider themselves Bethlehem people and use the town as a shopping and marketing centre. Their territory stretches over the Judaean Hills to the southeast of the town past Herod's great fortress Herodion, past Tekoa, birthplace of Amos, and down to the bitter waters of the Dead Sea. Some members of the tribe went to work in Kuwait in the 1950s and with the money that they sent back their relatives began to settle, some in a newly built village near Herodion, some in Bethlehem or Tekoa. The finding of the Dead Sea Scrolls by two of their number in 1947 also injected money into the tribe; but some of them are still nomadic and live the age-old way of life of the Bedouin.[33]

Tamar was used as a place name, and it is mentioned in the Bible as being on the eastern sea, that is, the Dead Sea. It was from a branch of Tamar's line that David was born after several generations, and after many more generations, Jesus. It is very possible that the Ta'amreh became Christian at the beginning of the era, and this would explain why they were not banished with the Jews by Hadrian. They are the best candidates we have for the Shepherds of the Nativity story, and they themselves support the idea that they were once Christian, pointing as evidence to the remains of the Byzantine church in Tekoa. Sadly, the lives of shepherds of the hills today – especially near Hebron – are filled with fear because of harassment from both settlers and Israeli soldiers. Despite being vulnerable as targets of snipers, they are still capable of practising traditional hospitality. Recently, two shepherds were shot at, but escaped.[34] Sadly, their donkey died. When found, the donkey was discovered to be carrying a kettle and means of making and offering tea – so much did hospitality mean to shepherds on the hillside, so rooted a part did it play in their lonely lives; but even this was taken away.

A *pedagogy of peace*

What links the people of Bethlehem of New Testament times and the Advent journey is a longing for peace, a longing for a way out of the harshness, bitterness and injustice that frames life in the West Bank, East Jerusalem and in Gaza, as well as the conflict – or fear of it – that haunts the wider context of the Middle East, Afghanistan and Iraq. For the Israeli people, the very harshness of the oppression being inflicted on the Palestinians is exacerbated by their own fear of loss of the land, complicated by the traumatized memory of the Holocaust and 2,000 years without a land of their own.

Luke, in his final sections of the infancy narratives (2.22–52), paves the way for his pedagogy of peace. First, he teaches us the vital role that wisdom has to play. Christ is a child of wisdom (2.52) and Mary of Nazareth, as we have noted, offers us a spirituality of contemplation, as one who contemplates and reflects on the meaning of events (2.51). So along with the prophetic inspiration of Isaiah, the figure of *hokmah*/Sophia/Wisdom is a guiding motif in our story.[35] This is not academic wisdom for its own sake but a deep discernment that draws on faith sources, all dimensions of living and lessons from the past drawn from within a commitment to the wellbeing of all people. A wisdom that is past- and future-oriented; a practical wisdom tapped into by ordinary people to sustain the dignity of ordinary living amid constant humiliation, then as well as now; a wisdom oriented to action, as John the Baptist's response to those who came for Baptism made clear.[36]

Second, Luke is under no illusion that the pathway to peace will not escape suffering. Zechariah proclaimed at the birth of John that our feet would be guided 'into the way of peace' (1.79). But 'a sword will pierce through your own soul', prophesied Simeon to Mary (2.35). The angels' promise of peace at the birth of this child would not be achieved through the conquest of Rome, as Jesus' followers hoped; but it would be accomplished by challenging the oppressive powers in a non-violent way – and by paying the price for this, even by giving one's life. Third, we learn about peace by practising peace as a chosen lifestyle. Living peace when there is no peace was the delusive practice that Jeremiah – followed by Martin Luther – lamented: 'They have healed the wound of my people lightly, saying "Peace, peace," when there is no peace' (Jer. 6.14). But who could comprehend what Jesus (and Jeremiah) meant by peace, now or then? And why were the disciples so slow to understand?

But the final ingredient in Luke's pedagogy is to tell us that joy will be the gift of embracing the way to peace. 'Great joy' was the message of the angels. The shepherds returned to the hills joyfully. We are not told of the joy of Mary and Joseph – and the Palestinian family whose home they shared at the birth – or the joy of Joseph's kinsfolk in Bethlehem. But joy will be evident in Luke's story, as it gathers momentum, even to its climax. John's Gospel, even though it gives no birth narrative, is also filled with this sense of joy. For him, it is not the birth of the child of peace that is the focus: it is more the glory, the wondrous fact of God-becoming-human, of the flesh-taking of the divine becoming God-with-us, Emmanuel: 'And the Word became flesh and dwelt among us, and we have beheld his glory, glory as of the only Son from the Father, full of grace and truth' (John 1.14).

And that joy is still experienced and lived out with determination by the people of Bethlehem. In their resistance to the occupation, harassment and control of so many aspects of their lives, people choose to keep festivals and saints' days with joy. The traditional singing and dancing, pride in cultural traditions and telling of stories is very much alive. The Wall is covered in graffiti of different kinds – some protesting, some poignant (such as 'I want my ball back') and some paintings of great beauty, of flowers and trees and scenes of play. But this should never be understood as acceptance of the status quo. A non-governmental organization (NGO) based in the Cultural Centre of Aida refugee camp stages plays and concerts at the Wall. In April 2008 there was an event aimed to overcome boundaries and build bridges, organized by the Peace House (Anastas House) in Bethlehem:

> Music crosses boundaries. On Thursday April 17 at sunset, the music event 'Carried by the Wind' by composer Merlijn Twaalfhoven will not only bridge the differences between different styles and cultures, but literally traverses the walls that separate inhabitants of Bethlehem from each other. About fifty singers, percussion and wind players of all ages are placed on rooftops near the separation wall at Rachel's Tomb. In this way, the music reaches out over the divide and connects people that were once neighbours.[37]

No one is romanticizing or idealizing the grim reality that the Wall and the occupation bring. Nor that, in the town of Jesus' birth, the Christian population is decreasing rapidly.[38] But just as Luke depicted the birth of the promised child as a sign of hope, of light in the darkness, a time when heaven and earth shared in rejoicing, and as the announcing of the beginning of an alternative way to live in the face of injustice, so the Christians of the Holy Lands and all peoples in solidarity with them, can reach across the ages, empowered by that same Gospel, in this threatened hour, when the very survival of the Palestinian people is at stake.

Two challenges emerge at this stage: how to live today so as to experience this gospel joy and wonder in celebrating the birth of Jesus this Christmas; and how to let the people of Bethlehem themselves be our guides in seeking peace. We shall tackle the second of these first.

Bethlehem's inspiration in peacemaking

> And so Mary gave birth to hope
> in uncertainty, darkness,
> journeying and exclusion;
> And the message of hope was heard
> by shepherds, out on the edge.
> And now hope is found
> in a vulnerable, helpless child.[39]

Auden's shepherds saw the journey as without end, but had been given a vision of hope. This birth of hope is the beacon light guiding our task. Our first guide is a peace activist, inspired by Gandhi (among others), who is director of a group – Wi'am – that tackles the task of peacemaking on a practical level. This is Zoughbi Zoughbi: at his Bethlehem centre he taught me on how many levels the struggle for peace must be worked for.[40] The guiding idea for him is *sulha*, meaning reconciliation. He feels he is working in a pressure-cooker situation, so great is the suppressed anger of the people. He too is inspired by the 'Nazareth Manifesto' (see the last section of Chapter 2), by the vision of a new kingdom, a new order that it proclaims: if restorative justice is the hope and task, *sulha* is the means to prevent people from being hysterical, or venting their frustrations in violence upon each other. *Sulha*, a traditional concept that dates back to pre-Arabic times, has both traditional and new elements.[41] Because a group of young people decided to light a humble candle rather than curse the darkness, a proactive step was taken by creating the Palestinian Conflict Resolution Center (Wi'am) as a community place. Concerned with the needs of the people, and by addressing them, Wi'am walks the road of community justice. At the same time, the team know that responding to the grassroots level without addressing issues of justice on a political level might be considered lost labour. Conflict resolution is a vehicle to strengthen the notion of community justice. The approach of Wi'am is one enabling the sharing of minds, hearts and resources with the people. As Zoughbi says: 'We have become like a sponge to absorb the anger and frustration of the people who come to talk to us, air it out over a cup of coffee!'

For the Wi'am team, *sulha* is the *presence* of justice, not only a form of conflict resolution. Adhering to the traditional ways of conflict resolution, they are also open to other experiences in the world to enrich the pursuit of justice. Synergy through creativity and innovation is what inspires – an affirmation of the rich heritage in Palestinian culture, coupled with openness for new ways, techniques and approaches from the four corners of the world that help to sustain and preserve the human dignity and the rights of people without infringing others' rights. *Sulha* could be summarized as meaning *talk about justice*: it involves redressing the injustices and correcting the wrongs rather than avenging them or taking revenge. Relative justice helps in social transformation, strengthening the fibre of the Palestinian people through pluralism. For Zoughbi, justice is a threefold word: it means justice for all, involving mediation and not arbitration,[42] reparation or compensation as a way to baptize the resolution to be everlasting,[43] and a quality of relationship which is the important investment looked for in settling conflicts. So *sulha* is not a single event but a process that might take days, months, or even years. It is a holistic, not superficial approach.[44] As he says:

> In Sulha, we are always on call; we work according to people's time and schedule. We work for the community, to the people and from the people. We don't only walk with them the extra mile but the tenth extra mile whenever is needed![45]

Zoughbi is a man always on the road, continually available to local people in the effort to solve their disputes and grievances. It is a timely reminder to us now, when in frustration with the wider picture (violence, hunger, unequal distribution of wealth or distrust of bankers), our anger gets vented on the domestic scene, or in other personal and community relationships. For the second time Gandhi is invoked in our journey. Whereas Gandhi reflects the same lifestyle of simplicity as we saw in the life of John the Baptist, for Zoughbi he is an inspiration for his non-violence. Very clear that there is a global collective responsibility to end the conflict, Zoughbi sees three aspects to this: Palestinians must struggle to get rid of the occupier; pro-peace activists in Israel must continue their preventive measures to stop themselves being occupiers; and outside powers should enhance non-violent means to end the struggle.

Gandhi's influence on Zoughbi is complex, and not purely as advocating non-violence. The example of South Africa is salutary, where the methods used to end Apartheid included both retaliatory and non-violent means. Whereas Zoughbi sees no F. W. de Klerk in Israel, he sees many Nelson Mandelas, but laments that the Churches are not as outspoken as they were in the case of Apartheid.[46]

For Zoughbi, the real strength of Gandhi's example lies in the connection between *sulha*, *swaraj* (Gandhi's idea of self-discipline and control) and *sumud* (the Palestinian concept of steadfastness, patience and perseverance).[47] Citing Thich Nhat Hanh, a famous Tibetan Buddhist spiritual leader, Zoughbi saw the challenge as 'how to transform the garbage of anger into flowers of compassion'. Although these qualities of perseverance and steadfastness are not often cited in agendas for freedom and transformation, they are vital ingredients on the journey to reconciliation, and vital for anyone on a spiritual journey. *Sulha* – again, the daily practice of reconciliation and forgiveness – does not sound a glamorous tool, but is the daily bread of a healing that nurtures hope. Zoughbi plunges to the roots that prevent us embracing the praxis of reconciliation: he cites a Filipino poet, in another article, in words that recall the Magnificat:

> Talk to us about reconciliation
> Only if you first experience
> the anger of our dying.
> Talk to us about reconciliation
> If your living is not the cause
> of our dying.
> Talk to us about reconciliation
> Only if your words are not products of your devious scheme
> to silence our struggle for freedom.
> Talk to us about reconciliation
> Only if your intention is not to entrench yourself
> more on your throne.
> Talk to us about reconciliation
> Only if you cease to appropriate all the symbols
> and meanings of our struggle.[48]

The light of Christmas, shining in the darkness, is what enables this journey and praxis of reconciliation to begin.

4

Gospel peacemaking and a lifestyle of non-violence – 'a little child shall lead them'[1]

This life is only possible in a state of peace, and there is a need for preparing the ground for peace at all levels. Without peace, the current situation is only going to get worse, as it undoubtedly can. Peace is not one-dimensional, it is a fabric that need[s] to be tightly woven and it is essential to weave it well . . . this means working for a self-sustainable peace, which completely ends every form of Israeli control over all Palestinian lives and lands occupied in 1967; *a peace that provides security, space and a viable future for both peoples.*[2]

Whatever house you enter, first say 'Peace be to this house!' And if there is a peace-person, your peace will rest upon this person. Otherwise it will return to you.[3]

> I seek peace, let me BE peace.
> I seek justice, let me be just.
> I seek a world of kindness, let me be kind.
> I seek a world of generosity, let me be generous with all that
>   I have and to everyone I encounter in my life and to those
>   whom I do not encounter but who need my help . . . *Let me*
>   *pass that love on to the next generations in an even fuller and*
>   *more conscious way.*[4]

As we near the end of this Advent journey, we ask how a theology of giving, initiated by God's love and generosity, can be realized in practice in this market-driven world. How can it become part of peacemaking and reconciliation? Rabbi Michael Lerner (cited above) calls for us to pass on love to the next generations, so we focus first on children, always central at Christmas, asking how celebrating the birth of the child of peace may offer a path forward from present excess to a different praxis. This may call for a radical re-education for which the path of non-violence holds out a beacon light.

The tears of Jesus: 'Would that even today you knew the things that make for peace!'[5]

Standing on the Mount of Olives and gazing towards the walls of the Old City – while recalling the grief of Jesus as he knew his message would be rejected, and realized the coming fate of the Holy City – is to experience deep sadness at the current impasse in peacemaking. The Golden Dome of the Rock – with the adjacent Al-Aqsa mosque – shines resplendent,[6] a brilliant reminder that this city is sacred for three faiths: near to it, with its own impressive dome, is the Church of the Holy Sepulchre, which together with Bethlehem and Nazareth is the most sacred pilgrimage site for Christians. It is thought that it stands on the site of Golgotha, where Jesus was crucified. Equally close is the Wailing Wall, its foundations once forming part of the Temple of Herod the Great. So important is possession of Jerusalem for the three faiths, and so contested is its identity, that discussion in the efforts to achieve peace is almost impossible. Haunting the life of Jesus, from Bethlehem to Galilee and on to Jerusalem, and prompting his grief, is the tragedy that the message of peace that would bring about a new social order was to be rejected. How could this grief be assuaged by the way we now approach Christmas? Peace has now to be worked for on many levels – as hinted at by the first of the quotations above. So first we tackle the problem of Christmas gift-giving from children's perspectives and expectations.

Children and the market: childhood's disenchantment

The focus on this issue arises because it is unrealistic to suppose one can move from the Christmas expectations of children, whipped up by the market and peer pressure, to an ethic and spirituality of simplicity that the gospel ethic encourages. First, we look at these pressures.

Children are adversely affected by the market in two ways: as victims and as consumers.[7] Because of the market's relentless pursuit of profit, children in many countries play a vital role as cheap labour. In fact, 250 million children worldwide are involved in labour, many of them in dangerous and exploitative conditions. In agricultural areas it is usually expected that children will help in the fields, will take care of sheep, goats and younger siblings – this affects girl-children specifically – so will inevitably miss out on schooling.

Whether we refer to the street children of Latin America, children exploited through paedophilia, trafficking and prostitution, children abused, children bringing up their siblings in AIDS-stricken Africa, children as refugees and asylum seekers, children denied education because of the need to work,[8] the global problems are devastating in their effects on children. A quick look at the websites of, for example, Christian Aid or Save the Children conveys the impression of determined and courageous efforts to remedy a situation spiralling out of control.

The following story illustrates the severity of the effects on children: a young East African woman, China Keitetsi (now 27), was born in a village near the south-western border, was cruelly treated by both father and stepmother and ran away from home at the age of nine. But she was found by look-out soldiers of the NRA, the guerrilla army of Yoweri Musuveni, now Uganda's president, and was forced, along with other children – as young as six – to become a soldier. They were given guns and told that the guns were their mothers. To lose or damage a gun carried penalties of beating, being rolled in the mud and ultimately the firing squad.[9] The army was her home until she was 19, when she escaped. Abused by officers, forced to have sex (China now has two children), the girls were forced by day to act like boys, but their roles were reversed at night. Many children did not survive – either they died in skirmishes or took their own lives. And there are an estimated 300,000 child soldiers across the world.

This story points to the diverse and often tragic realities of children's lives across the globe. Poverty, gender, wars, environmental disasters, caste and social position, lack of legal protection all determine the contours of a child's world. Now market forces, competition and profit are forcing half the world's children into degrading work, and the other half into consuming the products.

Children as consumers

This is the area that most concerns us in the fever of pre-Christmas spending: let us step into the brave new world of cyberspace:

> A child clicks an icon on her computer and is immediately transported to a richly graphic, brightly coloured, interactive children's playground on the World Wide Web. Bathed in psychedelic colours of hot pink, lime green, and lemon yellow, the site's home page serenades with whimsical tunes and beckons with vibrant flashing signs. 'Bug your buddies with creepy-crawly e-cards made by you,' says one. 'Zap your friends with Wacky DigSig cards made by Fruit Gushers and Fruit Roll-ups,' urges another. One click on 'play', another on 'buzz', and the child is invited to display her own artwork in 'Kids' Gallery, or 'hang-out' with the site's web characters, Devin, Jessie and Zach.[10]

It is unquestionable that these interactive features have an enormous, rich potential for education. The concern is children's vulnerability to commercial pressures that they present, and the effect this has on their worlds and expectations of spending. In the Western world a growing number of children have access to their own personal media devices. Research shows that time spent in front of the TV is declining whereas time spent in front of the computer is shooting up: time spent online has increased exponentially with the arrival of interactive sites like Facebook and Twitter.

Sociological and demographic factors (including divorce) have combined to produce a situation in which children's spending power has increased: children under 12 now control or influence the spending of almost $500 billion. A new kind of marketing – called interactive and 'relational' – has become interwoven with children's online culture. Despite legal attempts to curb the pressures on children, the potential of engaging and compelling one-to-one marketing is growing. It is not just that advertising is woven into children's content areas, but that in many cases *the product is the content.* Barbi.com would be a good example, where a personalized Barbie can be made and purchased for a particular child. Commercial sites now deliberately hone in on a child's developmental needs, such as the need to belong. According to J. U. McNeal:

> The belonging (affiliation) need, which causes us to seek cooperative relations, is very strong in children . . . Also children are looking for order in their lives. There are so many things to encounter that some order is necessary to cope with them all. A trusting relationship in which satisfying acquisitions can always be expected helps to give order to an increasingly complex life.[11]

It is not only belonging that is vulnerable to commercial pressures. Increasingly storytelling is also being targeted: narrative strands within a programme will lead viewers to a 'buying opportunity' and then return them to the story after a purchase.[12]

One website offers replicas of furniture, clothing, cars and other producers from such popular (US) teen shows as *Charmed* and *Seventh Heaven*. Viewers go to the website, click on a photo of the house used in the show, then the room, then on an item within it. If, for example, this is a rug, the customer is immediately hot-linked to the retailer's website, where the rug can be purchased. The fact that this is steadily increasing means that if the internet is to succeed in offering a rich and diverse educational environment for children, legal safeguards, policies to curtail marketing abuses, commercial-free sites and a debate as to what quality programmes for children should contain, are all urgent.[13]

The effect of interactive marketing on children has here only been seen from a Western perspective: but expensive Western toys also appear inevitably in the markets of poor countries: a dependency culture may be fostered here by the advertising strategies of global corporations. The distinguished Nigerian author, Wole Soyinka, speaks of African children lured or coerced 'to develop an incurable dependency syndrome and consume themselves to death'.[14]

Caught in the global web of consumerism, the self-respecting youth dare not be seen without a Walkman – more recently, an i-Pod – with often devastating consequences.[15] The result is that children in marginal cultures in Africa are left 'at the mercy of the McDonaldised, standardised or routinised information, education, games and other entertainment burgers served in the interests of profit by the global corporate media'.[16]

That religion, too, is prey to the market I illustrate here from a Jewish context. Susan Linn, author of *Consuming Kids*, recalls that Primo Levi titled his early-1980s novel of resistance to the Holocaust, *If Not*

Now, When?, and how the slogan was taken up by Civil Rights leaders calling for an end to segregation, as well as Czech students in fomenting the 1989 Velvet Revolution. But in 2005 it was introduced into a campaign to sell 'Black Pepper Jack', a flavour of Doritos tortilla chips. This was an integrated campaign using cell phones, TV, radio, billboards and the internet, with the message of the purpose-built 'inNw?' ('If not now, when?') website: 'Livin' life in the now. Don't procrastin8. Don't hesit8. And bring a bag of Doritos with you.' As Linn puts it, a phrase tying Judaism to social action will for children now forever mean Doritos![17]

Small wonder that children, caught up in these pressures from an early age, are not going to be satisfied with one simple gift under the tree on Christmas morning![18] To discover some answers, let us listen to the voices of children themselves.

What do children really want?

Children, like adults, can be caught in the market's all-encompassing, addictive web of shopping for fashion, toys and fast food. In its merciless targeting of comparatively powerless young people, in its deliberate 'Disneyfication' of human yearnings and the cult of celebrity, childhood itself has been disenchanted, its very existence threatened. How can an Advent journey wanting to enter more deeply into the Mystery of Incarnation cope with these realities?

If children themselves are given a chance to say what they really want, what do they say? This example comes from an initiative of children from four European countries who came together in Scotland in 1992 for the first Children's EcoCity project (out of which was born, for Scotland at least, a Children's Parliament that still exists). These children identified the most important areas that children cared about as being:

- identity and belonging;
- feeling safe and being cared for;
- freedom;
- caring for our environment;
- having our say.[19]

The achievement of these children, at the third EcoCity project in 1996, was to design – imaginatively and creatively – a model eco-city in the Craigmillar area of Edinburgh they called 'Castlevale'. The values witnessed to in the project were, for example, cooperative learning by executing a project together, and support for environmental education.[20]

The second example is Oxfam's International Youth Partnership (OIYP – the 'P' originally stood for 'Parliament'), which is now ten years old. It involves 145 partners in 61 countries. These young people, largely from poor cultures, highlight issues more related to sheer survival, like access to water and the violence inflicted on their sense of security. They are concerned about the lack of education, about the vulnerability of young people in agriculture, about the trafficking of young girls and about human rights.[21]

Both of the groups in these examples wanted to be listened to and were eager to have a voice.

Any attempt to reimagine childhood with gospel values has to begin from a real-life context: it cannot ignore the children of sectarian Belfast, the militarized child soldiers of Africa, the shell-shocked children of Gaza or the children forced to play in the shadow of the Wall in the West Bank. Yet even when people are living in fear or dire poverty, continually hungry, they can still practise great generosity and hospitality – deeply rooted religious values.[22]

Perhaps curiosity, play, joy in the present and sense of adventure, together with qualities like belief in magic and enchantment, a sense of awe and wonder, love of secret hiding spaces ('making camps') and an ability to form special relationships with birds and animals come to mind as integral to childhood.[23] If adults can create the conditions and safe spaces for children to experience authentic childhood (and not be forced into becoming soldiers, or suffering abuse in so many ways), they themselves might be shown the way back to healing, reconciling relationships, including attitudes to the earth that would prohibit wastefulness and devastation. The story of *The Secret Garden* is symbolic of such reconciling possibility.[24] Through the relationship with growing things and tending plants and trees, and the guidance of the earth child, Dickon, the spoilt children Mary and Colin – who is disabled – become transformed, and Colin learns to walk again.

'Mary! Dickon!', he cries, 'I can walk . . . And I shall live for ever and ever.' 'Beginning from now,' added the theologian Rosemary Haughton, evoking both that joyful sense of the present as well as the sense of expectation of *happy ever after* that informs Christian eschatology.[25] It is also part of Advent hope.

The once-and-future child

It is highly likely that the child, victim both of the world's violence and today's market pressures, was in the mind of Jesus, when he cried: 'Let the children come to me; do not hinder them, for to such belongs the kingdom of God. Truly, I say to you, whoever does not receive the kingdom of God like a child shall not enter it' (Mark 10.14–15). What we do know is that Jesus' proclamation of the kingdom – especially as presented in Mark's Gospel, written, it is thought, at the time of the Jewish uprising against the Romans[26] – is a subversive programme for a new socio-cultural order, where the least would be the greatest and the dominant coercive power of the mighty would be overturned, not by a rival power, but by an alternative way of living and a different imagining of power.[27] This, we saw, was the inspiration of the Magnificat,[28] and we have suggested that the seeds of this vision would have been sown in Jesus' mind by Mary of Nazareth.

Children were the least of the least in New Testament society. Without legal protection, the comparison with child labourers or street children comes to mind. Poor children were always hungry and forced into begging; they were not far from exploited children of today, especially of criminalized youngsters organized into gangs: the picture has not changed much through the centuries. Charles Dickens poignantly described the misery of children in nineteenth-century England and their powerlessness in a cruel system.

Jesus now lifts children from the edges and places them centre stage, in the midst of the newly forming beloved community. The message here is not so much that everyone must be childlike, that adulthood is displaced, but that the child commands attention as standing first in the cycle of violence and oppression.[29] Ched Myers cites the work of the psychoanalyst Alice Miller, who shows how this process, the 'silent drama of the child', works: the adult humiliated and abused as a child goes on to humiliate and abuse – so the cycle becomes intergenerational and *psychically enforced*. We have become increasingly aware that the growing instances of teenagers – and even younger children – killing is related to intergenerational neglect, many-levelled deprivation, and cruelty sometimes on an unimaginable level.

As Myers rightly observes,[30] we cannot make too close parallels between contemporary violence and family and cultural patterns in New Testament times, yet Jesus' radical gesture can still be an invitation to build an alternative regime of justice and peace, where the most vulnerable categories of people are privileged and where non-violence as life-stance is chosen over violent military retaliation. Highlighting children and placing them centrally is an indication that the alternative teaching and lifestyle of non-violence must begin with family life.

Gospel peace and the stance of non-violence

In Chapter 1, the lifestyle of non-violence in the person of John the Baptist was introduced, especially in his austerity and his choice of simplicity. Non-violence was expressed in the simplicity of his way of existence in the wilderness as well as in his response to the crowds who flocked to him. The comparison between John the Baptist and Gandhi was also introduced. Here – and as I write it is the 140th anniversary of the birth of the Mahatma[31] – the link with Gandhi is again invoked, this time because of the radicality of Jesus' non-violent proclamation of the kingdom and its link with Gandhi's project. Within this vision lies the hope of re-education of society, beginning with children. A spirituality of simplicity of lifestyle finds a home within this vision.

With Gandhi it is possible to glimpse the same revisioning of family life and community that is evident in the Gospels. As in the Gospels, Gandhi's revisioning of the family from the narrow kinship model to the open household (where blood ties give way to the ties of those committed to kingdom values),[32] as well as his ashrams (a form of committed, disciplined community), can be seen as a programme for the transformation of relationships from the systemic to the personal. The aim was to address the deeply rooted insidious patterns of domination – in his case the might of the British Empire, and some of the hierarchical structures of Indian society. Again, this is exactly what is envisaged by the Gospels' notion of the kingdom of God.[33] Even if he was, eventually, unsuccessful in his own times, Gandhi tried to tackle the worst example of oppression of his age – that of Untouchability – by insisting that everyone shared the humblest of tasks, even the cleaning of toilets,[34] which was strongly resisted by the higher castes. But it is particularly in his idea of *satyagraha* as a strategy of non-violent action that the best comparison lies.[35] *Satyagraha* – the power of truth – was the method by which Gandhi tried to embody his vision of *swaraj*, translated variously as 'discipline', 'self-control', 'freedom' or 'liberation'. The appeal of truth had been central for Gandhi since his childhood. For John's Gospel, 'truth' is a central value, as Jesus promises that he will send his followers the 'Spirit of Truth' and prays that their fledgling community will be 'consecrated in truth'.[36]

Satyagraha is sometimes erroneously described as 'passive resistance', but Gandhi is referring to something far more active, namely non-violent resistance to an oppressive regime. Its *active* character and link with the New Testament come from the style of ministry of Jesus and his disciples: they engage in healing, compassionate actions, speaking and judging with the authority not of military might, but of a truth they ground in the vision of the kingdom of peace and justice. All the actions Jesus took were trying to undermine exploitative economic and political structures. For example, the Salt March (against an unjust tax)[37] and his fast-unto death have to be put in the context of offering an alternative way of living. And this is the way he is remembered by numerous groups today in India, whether they, formally speaking, are Gandhians or not.

I suggest that this is the way we should understand the ever-present concern in the Gospels with peace – that actually it is a constant stance of non-violence that is being advocated. And as Gandhi said, *we have to begin with the children* . . . This is why the daily practices in the Ashrams, beginning with morning spinning (in which he participated), were so important. Children were to live the realities of non-violence from their waking moments. Gandhi paid particular attention to the education of children – and along with that, of women.[38]

The Gospel's urgent cry for peace

Next, I look at the constant gospel call to peacemaking, within a non-violent stance and the call to an alternative way of living. We have seen that the births of the two children, John and Jesus, were heralded with hopes of peace. But what could be the explanation for the cry of Simeon in the temple – 'Lord, now you are letting your servant depart in peace, according to your word' (Luke 2.29) – when he caught sight of the infant Jesus for the first time? Yes, Simeon can now meet death with peace, but there is more to it. In recognizing who Jesus is, Simeon experiences a conviction of the fulfilment of Israel's hopes and a sense of a new beginning; a sense of the profundity of what Luke means by peace. He certainly does not mean what the Romans mean by peace. In the end this rather mystical meaning of peace may turn out to be the most crucial aspect of Luke's theology of peace, and the most linked with Advent expectations of a redeemed future.

Fast-forward to the end of Jesus' earthly life: it is striking that at his arrest in Gethsemane, after the incident of the cutting off of the ear of Malchus, the servant of the High Priest (narrated by all four evangelists), only Luke tells us that Jesus said, '"No more of this!" And he touched his ear and healed him' (Luke 22.51).[39] *The new order is not to be attained through violence.* Peace is linked with the theme of journeying, which for the Synoptic Gospels (most clearly in Luke) is always towards Jerusalem and the fulfilling of Jesus' divinely sent mission. The two main Lukan Gospel frames – the Bethlehem journey (Luke 2) and the journey to Emmaus (Luke 24) – both point to the special spiritual significance of journeying. His Gospel is also a Gospel of repentance, so journeying, as is already clear, involves 'turning' and repenting – the first step that we made on this Advent journey.

Peace is also a vital ingredient in the sending of the 72 disciples on their mission journeys. Both Matthew and Luke stress that they are to bring peace to the households they visit, and expect to receive it in the mutuality of hospitality, so important to Middle-Eastern culture.[40] This is confirmed by the reference to Sodom in the same passage: Jesus' disciples would remember that Scripture taught that it was the sin of Sodom that brought down God's wrath on the city (Genesis 19), and this sin was the violation of hospitality inflicted on the messengers of God.[41] But peacemaking is firmly placed within the vision of the kingdom of God, a link that is picked up by many peace groups on our contemporary scene. The healing of sickness and restoration of health are always close to the heart of Jesus, as well-being of the whole person is linked with justice: healing events are often accompanied by the injunction to 'go in peace' – as with the healing of the haemorrhaging woman and the woman of the town who is forgiven because she loves so much (Luke 7.50; 8.40–56).[42]

Now we explore the link between peace and the forgiveness of sins. Peace must mean far more than simply 'peace of mind' – as with the woman healed of the issue of blood just mentioned. That is but one dimension. The healing the woman experienced must be linked with a wholeness that restored her dignity as a human being. Again, the despised and marginalized of society are restored to a central place in the new order, where forgiveness, the flowing generosity of God, a culture of grace, replaces one of dominance and violence.

The most significant teaching of a non-violent, subversive order is seen in the Sermon on the Mount (Luke 6; Matt. 5). Here non-violence, love, forgiveness and generosity are urged strongly: 'Love your enemies, do good to those who hate you, bless those who curse you, pray for those who abuse you. To one who strikes you on the cheek, offer the other also' (Luke 6.27–29); 'But love your enemies, and do good, and lend, expecting nothing in return' (Luke 6.35). Non-violent peacemaking is the striking feature here. Yet the picture of the Synoptic Gospels needs to be scrutinized with a gender lens. Even though Luke – and Matthew to a lesser extent – do give emphasis to the participation of women in the Jesus movement, we could not expect them to have the same sensitivity that is required today. How could we tell a woman experiencing continual, severe domestic violence to 'turn the other cheek'?! How could we expect a family that has been forced out of bed at 4 a.m. to face the demolition of their home in front of their eyes to 'love their enemy'? In exploring a theology of non-violence in the life of Jesus, it is important to recognize a certain (time-bound) androcentric character within the Sermon on the Mount. As Luise Schottroff writes:

81

> It is not enough to situate a story of women's resistance next to the androcentric Sermon on the Mount and its androcentric interpretation, even when the latter is conceived in terms of a praxis of peace. Both the sermon and its interpretation need to be submitted to a critique of patriarchy, since otherwise they would carry on women's oppression into the work of peace, usually without knowing it.[43]

Thus even non-violent resistance is not immune to sexist oppression, and needs to be subjected to this critical lens.

Yet later, in 12.51, Luke presents us with a shocking statement that on the surface seems far away from non-violent resistance: 'Do you think that I have come to bring peace on earth? No, I tell you, but rather division.' Luke then chronicles all the social relations that will be divided. This is where we see the radicality and eschatological nature of the path to peace. We know that Jesus has come to bring peace, because the angelic message was clear, as well as the consistency of his teaching. But Jesus faced huge blockages to peace that could be symbolically described as demons. The word 'demon' or 'devil' has the Greek root *diabolos*, meaning dividing, splitting. Jesus is pitted against the forces splitting society apart.[44] A culture of peace is no cosy tea-party! It even involves anger at the evil to be resisted. Normally one cites Jesus being angry when he casts out the money-changers in the temple (Luke 19.45–46), but here we can also read blazing anger: 'I came to cast fire on the earth, and would that it were already kindled!' (12.49).

Anger and grief are integral parts of a subversive theology working for action and change. In this stage of Jesus' life, the spiritual journey is not metaphorical, but to Jerusalem, with intimations of persecution and the radicality of the demands of the coming kingdom. Conflicts between kingdom values and those of the world are unavoidable when one is given a new and transforming way to live:

> When He called His society together Jesus gave its members a new way of life to live. He gave them a new way to deal with offenders – by forgiving them . . . He gave them a new way to deal with money – by sharing it . . . He gave them a new way to deal with a corrupt society – by building a new order, not smashing the old. He gave them a new pattern of relationship between parent and child, between master and slave, in which he made concrete a radical vision of what it means to be a human person. He gave them a new attitude toward the state and to the 'enemy nation.'[45]

A recent interpretation of the Sermon on the Mount suggests an active form of resistance that fits well with the visions of both Jesus and Gandhi. The heart of the matter is about what kind of power governs kingdom relationships. Relational power, the power of mutuality (which is how we characterized the Annunciation moment), is fragile. But Gandhi's life and development of non-violent resistance showed that relational power has the power of truth. In his *satyagraha* movement, he attempted to reach the heart of his opponent:

> Let my friend understand the implications of non-violence. It is a process of conversion . . . But there is no such thing as compulsion in the scheme of non-violence. Reliance has to be placed upon the ability to reach the intellect and the heart . . . Its secret lies in bearing anything that may be inflicted on us . . . We want to win, not by striking terror in the ruler, but by awakening their sense of justice.[46]

'Awakening their sense of justice' is a non-violent method, but also a high form of action, far from a sense of passive resistance. This message was inspired by the Sermon on the Mount:[47] but even if Palestinian Christians and peace activists today are inspired by Gandhi, theirs is always a specific contextual interpretation. Justice, mercy and loving kindness go alongside the way to reconciliation and forgiveness. For Archbishop Elias Chacour, whose village (Ibillin) is very close to the Mountain where the Sermon is thought to have taken place, and who, since childhood, has taken refuge there in search of inspiration, the words 'Blessed are the peacemakers' should be understood in a very active way. He says that the word 'blessed' – Greek *makarioi* – is derived from the Aramaic *ashray* (verb: *yashar*). This has an active meaning: 'Set yourself on the right way for the right goal; to turn around, repent.'[48]

Sabeel[49] never separates forgiveness from justice. At the seventh Sabeel International Conference in 2008, on *al-Nakba*,[50] participants heard the remarkable story of the former Jewish soldier, Josef Ben-Eliezer, present with his son and daughter-in-law. Himself a Holocaust survivor, he had fled to Israel and joined the Irgun, one of the groups responsible for the early massacres dispossessing Palestinians from their villages. Involved in the rounding up of the Arabic men of the village of Al-Tantura, he suddenly experienced a moment of déjà vu, as he remembered his own experience of being rounded up in a square in Germany. Years of seeking his own spiritual pathway ended in conversion to Christianity and his joining the Bruderhof, an international Peace Group, whose English base is at Robertsbridge, north of Hastings.[51] Later, through searching the internet, he discovered the names of the sons of the men killed at Al-Tantura, and journeyed to Israel to beg forgiveness. His journey seeking forgiveness and reconciliation carries on.

It is easy to dismiss the impact of one incident. What does it mean, in the face of intransigent violent policies? Does it stop the expansion of settlements, or harassment of Palestinian school children trying to get to school?

Mitri Raheb, Lutheran pastor in Bethlehem,[52] gives an example of non-violent resistance undertaken by a whole village, namely Beit Sahour (near Bethlehem – the site of the Shepherds' Field). The villages wanted to join in Palestinian resistance during the Intifada by refusing to pay their taxes. They had received no social services, not a single benefit from paying tax. The Israeli Defense Force (IDF) decided to 'teach them a lesson', and completely surrounded the village, cutting them off from the rest of the world. Then the soldiers began to cart off material goods from their houses – TV sets, fridges, washing machines and so on. One story is extremely poignant. The soldiers removed everything from the living room of one house:

> Each piece of furniture called up stories, reminiscences and the memory of the sweat it had cost them. After a few hours, the living room was totally empty. The soldiers, having robbed her of all her possessions, turned to bid farewell to the elderly owner, a Christian. The old woman looked at the young soldier sadly. Her glance contained suffering, pain, and rage. Her lips moved, but not to curse, not to cry out, not even to scold.
>
> 'You forgot the curtains. Please do not forget to take them down too and remove them.'
>
> An eerie silence descended on the room. Shamed and guilty the soldiers left. They took everything except the curtains.[53]

The elderly woman had retained her dignity. This was the kind of non-violent resistance the Sermon on the Mount was speaking about in saying: 'And if anyone would sue you and take your tunic, let him have your cloak as well' (Matt. 5.40).

If such non-violent resistance is for the long haul, without apparent political success in the short term (we cannot judge its moral success), how do the people retain courage and hope? There is a remarkable spirituality developing in Palestine, the spirituality of *sumud*, or steadfastness. Jean Zaru writes of its importance: 'To practice *sumud* is to remain steadfast on one's own land . . . to remain steadfast in service to one's homeland to the struggle for freedom.'[54] In her book, *Occupied with Nonviolence*, she gives a remarkable example of women's peaceful resistance in the refugee camps in Ramallah. Punished by having gas and electricity supplies cut off, the women tried to find ways of baking bread by collecting wood and rubbish and making a communal fire. But the soldiers came and tried to put the fire out and destroy the dough. The women resisted, shouting:

> Go tell your leaders that no matter what you do, no matter what kind of restrictions you impose on us, we will not allow our children to starve. We will find a way to bake bread, and all your efforts to destroy our spirits are not going to succeed. What God has created no one can destroy![55]

This is *sumud*, she concludes.

The spirituality of *sumud* brings together many of the aspects of a praxis of reconciliation, of living out a relational theology seeking justice. Spirituality in its simplest meaning is the life of the Spirit, embracing the human spirit, human zeitgeist (spirit of the times), the energy grounding hope, itself linking with the divine, the universal spirit of life that is shared by all faiths. But the meaning of spirit that unites us in the most literal way is the Spirit as breath of life grounding hope. Taking a deep breath, in this, the dark night of the Palestinian people, and many peoples in the Middle East, means connecting with this Spirit, calling on resources for the long haul, refusing to give way to the suffocating effects of daily humiliation. No easy option. Drawing deep on the Spirit, breath of life, is keeping hope alive.

And taking a deep breath brings the gift of *living peacefully when there is no peace*. This means calling on a type of imagination that is prophetic in remembering and seeing differently, an imagination that summons us to live out of a new reality that does not yet exist – but can be embodied in every act of non-violent resistance, of giving thanks, giving God praise, in acts of simple kindness, moments of joy, beauty, singing and dancing. In so doing strength is drawn from ancient traditions that form Palestinian identity, such as hospitality, love of the beauty of the land, the myths and poems that celebrate this, the stories that children will remember. In times of persecution, tensions and daily harassment, it is even more important to draw strength from cherished traditions.[56]

Mitri Raheb stresses the importance of culture for Palestinian contextual theology as well as for a spirituality of *sumud*:

> Culture becomes thus the space where people can meet others and themselves, where they can discover a language that is local yet universal, and where they realize that in order to breathe, one has to keep windows wide open to new winds and fresh air brought across the seas and oceans.[57]

Toine van Teeffelen and Fuad Giacaman see the importance of *sumud* for a theology and spirituality of non-violent resistance. Historically, in 1978 the term was given to a fund in Jordan that collected contributions from Arab countries to support the conditions of Palestinians in the occupied territories. Since then it has passed through several meanings and come to symbolize the value of staying put while confronting an overwhelmingly stronger military and political force. Raja Shehadeh, a lawyer from Ramallah, has giving the concept two important meanings – roughly speaking, an exterior and interior interpretation. On the one hand, the *samid*, or steadfast one, refuses to accept being dominated by the occupation; on the other hand, he or she refuses to become dominated by feelings of revenge and hatred of the enemy. *Sumud* becomes used as an umbrella term for stories of daily life under the occupation that emphasize love of the land and its beauty. Yet 'staying put' should be seen more as imaginative resistance, challenging the spirit to move on, 'crossing boundaries along alternate routes, despite pains and sacrifices'.[58] This is reminiscent of the New Testament context where Jesus, who in the context of warning his followers of the great persecutions that are to come, yet tells them not to fear: 'But not a hair of your head will perish. By your endurance you will gain your lives' (Luke 21.19–19).[59]

The final dimension of the spirituality of *sumud* is the dimension of vision. All writers cited are eloquent in their hopes for a land shared peacefully between two peoples and an end to occupation and the sharing of Jerusalem. They call on a vision of the Holy Spirit as beauty to sustain this hope and the reality of struggle. Beauty is linked with the holy and the truthful, and possesses a unique power to move hearts. The challenge for the moral imagination of a theology of non-violence is to transcend narrow, deadlocked views, while still living amid cycles of violence, building on people's participation and creating spaces for authentic renewed relationships of trust. As Gandhi saw, the need for a spiritual practice is crucial – one that respects both the depth of woundedness but also the need for daily strength just to survive. Deep in all faith traditions there are in fact resources for coping with poverty, pain and the trauma of violence. It is also through the Spirit that we are enabled to *inhabit the truth of the other – and to respect difference* in the formation of communities across the boundaries of faith and nation, the valuing of particularity and specificity. This had been Gandhi's vision in his efforts to unite Hindus and Muslims. The Spirit is a great *boundary-crosser*. Through the Spirit comes the strength to live peace when there is no peace and to live from a new reality that does not yet exist – *exactly what we do at Christmas*. So taking the long breath of *sumud* means sharing God's own steadfastness, compassion and vulnerability – which brings us back to the birth of the child.

Returning to the child

> But little did the Infant Dream
> That all the Treasures of the World were by:
> And that Himself was so the Cream
> And Crown of all, which round about did lie.[60]

The poet, Thomas Traherne, evokes the consciousness of every child – here I evoke a double meaning: this Bethlehem-born child has a unique relationship to the creation that surrounds him.

We have travelled some way from the child's expectation of presents on Christmas morning. I have suggested that children cannot be expected to move from the overwhelming commercial pressures to a simpler lifestyle and a non-violent vision of the world unless this is placed within a wider vision that attracts them.

At a primal level the entire earth is God's gift to us – *Gaia* is gift, as Anne Primavesi expressed it.[61] Even if economic systems have persuaded us that the market economy is the primary reality, we live within God's gift economy, as we prepare for the great giving at Christmas. At Christmas the overwhelming generosity of God becomes incarnate in human flesh. This is why the 'Christian Midnight' is such a solemn moment. *Above all, the feast of giving celebrates God's giving.* So how could our gift-giving and feasting mirror this appropriately, celebrating God's gift economy without falling into an extravagant excess? Miroslav Volf gives a clue, imagining an ideal scene around the Christmas tree, when shopping is over:

> thoughtfully chosen gifts are strewn under the Christmas tree, and the long-awaited ritual begins. Each person gives, and each receives. No one gives first, so that others feel obliged to reciprocate; all give and receive at the same time, or rather, each receives in turn so that all can rejoice with one another. Each is grateful, each is generous, and all are rejoicing in each other's joy. Gifts . . . are sacraments of love, both divine and human.[62]

Readers might react that this is an ideal for another world! Yet Volf helpfully expands the notion of giving, from the immediate circle to towards enabling others to give.[63] How can this giving – at the heart of Christmas meaning and practice – become part of *forgiving*, the way to peace and reconciliation in our world?

A deeper vision will attract children, first, if it attracts their parents and friends and meshes with their own deepest longings. Children usually love adventure and stories of heroism – and these abound in peace movements. Children, as Traherne's poem suggests, are capable of a sustaining relationship with nature, and often become angry at the exploitation of the earth as seen from their own perspective. They are able to act in courageous ways themselves, as numerous contemporary stories from conflict situations across the world relate. The 'restorying' of Christmas to reflect the inspiration of children today is one way forward. Matthew (18.10), in his version of Jesus' placing children central, remarks that, 'in heaven their angels always see the face of my Father who is in heaven'. Restorying Christmas – beyond Disneyfied Santa Claus and his reindeer – is an opportunity to let the innocence, trust and vulnerability of children and young people be taken seriously by the shapers of culture. It is to present the challenge of linking the vulnerability of the birth of the Christchild with the vulnerable situation of children worldwide, through a storytelling that leads to action, especially to action for peace and reconciliation.

Finally a story from Bethlehem that makes this link in a poignant way: it is a story that emerged during the second Intifada (2000). In the Peace House at Bethlehem, a woman related how she, four months pregnant with her first child (she had already lost a first baby), was returning from Mass at the Church of the Nativity with her husband when, driving through Manger Square, their car was caught between Palestinian stone-throwers and Israeli soldiers throwing tear-gas grenades. She was overcome with fumes and had to close the car windows. Sadly, she had to be taken to hospital in the night and lost this baby too. She was still grieving when, some months later, she was in Jerusalem, in a large store. While ascending on an escalator she saw a young Jewish couple with a baby in a buggy. The buggy was tipping over and the baby about to fall out down the escalator. She thought, 'I want that Jewish child to die – in return for my baby.' What she actually did was to warn the young mother and save the baby. The couple were overcome with gratitude and she was able to explain her feelings – one generous gesture in a praxis of reconciliation.[64]

The link between Christmas and peace can be made by journeying through the Peace Gardens, an initiative of Pax Christi that especially involves children. There is now a network of Peace Gardens in the UK – with special focus on children's exploration. As with *The Secret Garden* cited above, the link between children and nature is also an important dimension of Christmas preparation. Issues such as the number of fir trees that must be cut down, the number of turkeys consumed – these often concern children more than adults.

Placing children centre stage, not just for gift-giving and storytelling but for non-violent action for peace as well, is not only being faithful to the New Testament inspiration of the Beloved community, or to Gandhi's Ashram communities, but also recalls the prophet Isaiah's vision of new creation. His words are shining stars for us through the Advent and Christmas journey:

The wolf shall dwell with the lamb, and the leopard shall lie down with the young goat, and the calf and the lion and the fattened calf together; *and a little child shall lead them.* The cow and the bear shall graze; their young shall lie down together; and the lion shall eat straw like the ox. The nursing child shall play over the hole of the cobra, and the weaned child shall put his hand on the adder's den. (Isa. 11.6–8)

With the leitmotiv of the child, symbol of healed creation, our Advent journey has now brought us to the celebration of the feast, to Christmas Day.

5

Christmas Day – celebrating the feast

Of what happened later in the evening nothing definite can here be stated. None of the guests later had any clear remembrance of it. They only knew that the rooms had been filled with a heavenly light, as if a small number of halos had blended into one glorious radiance. Taciturn old people received the gift of tongues; ears that for years had been almost deaf were opened to it. Time itself had merged into eternity. Long after midnight the windows of the house shone like gold, and golden song flowed out into the winter air.[1]

In this vignette the writer, Isak Dinesen, evokes the near-magical quality of the special feast that took place in a small Norwegian hamlet where relationships between inhabitants had become sour and embittered. It introduces the theme of this chapter and the last stage of the Advent–Christmas journey: how the celebration of the Christmas feast and the experience of the hospitality of the 12-day season con- tribute to the praxis of reconciliation and peacemaking. In 'Babette's Feast', the alchemy was achieved by the artistry of the Parisian cook, Babette: this feast comprised the essential elements of festival noted by Harvey Cox in his book, *The Feast of Fools*, namely '*conscious excess, celebrative affirmation and juxtaposition*'.[2] By 'conscious excess' is meant that we deliberately choose to eat out-of-the-ordinary foods and enjoy special drinks (in this case, Babette spent her entire legacy!); in 'celebrative affirmation' we are doing more than marking an occasion (in the story it was the celebration of the anniversary of the founder of a special religious group), rather we affirm both the joyous or solemn rhythms of living and our love for friends and community; and in 'juxtaposition' it is made clear that this festive meal is in total contrast with normal fare and normal behaviour. That is what happened with 'Babette's Feast': this grimly austere Calvinist community had never tasted any more exotic food than a piece of haddock and a slice of bread as their daily fare. What they experienced in this extraordinary meal brought them to a new level of living and loving, broke them out of the pettiness that had become their accepted way of behaving, and enabled them to rediscover harmony and reconciliation. 'Did not our hearts burn within us . . . ?' cried the disciples after the Emmaus meal with Jesus (Luke 24.13–35), alluding to the deeper level of joy that his interpretation of the Scriptures concerning his death had given them: this reached a climax in the shared meal, and gives us a clue we shall follow. Was it not a similar radiance that emanated from the meal that St Francis of Assisi shared – a very rare occurrence – with St Clare at the Church of St Mary of the Angels outside Assisi?

> But at the first course St Francis began to speak about God in such a sweet and holy and profound way that he himself and St Clare and her companion and all the others who were at that poor little table were rapt in God by the overabundance of Divine grace that descended upon them.[3]

So great was the radiance emanating between the two saints that the good folk of Assisi thought that the church was on fire, rushed to extinguish the flames, only to find Francis and Clare 'rapt in God by contemplation and invested with power from on high'! So intense was the communication between the two that they paid little attention to the material food. Even allowing for hagiographical exaggeration, this story focuses on the quality and intensity of interaction that can happen at meals that evoke past traditions and future hopes. This is also a phenomenon of Jesus' sharing of meals with his disciples and even the crowds: it is the quality of lifting the occasion out of the ordinary level of experience that is glimpsed with the diversity of meals that Jesus shares with his followers in the Gospels, which climax in the farewell meal with the apostles before his death[4] – *when peace became the parting gift of Jesus*. In this, the last step of the Advent journey, we explore the inbuilt potential for peacemaking in the celebration of the Christmas feast. Each chapter has been steadily building up elements of a spirituality of peacemaking and reconciliation: moving through lifestyle practices of repentance and conversion to the earth, of watching and waiting, paying attention to the lived experience of ordinary life, and then of practising reconciliation in our own multiple life contexts, of simplicity and staying steadfast (the spirituality of *sumud*), we are ready to experience hospitality as the great celebratory practice of Christmas.

Hospitality – the yeast that binds

Traditions of hospitality bind together this chapter in a more profound way than a focus simply on the Christmas meal. The first link is with the culture of Middle-Eastern hospitality, even more crucial in a situation of scarcity and hunger, as is now the case in Gaza. What is meant here is not simply that hospitality is important in contemporary Palestine or throughout the entire Middle East; or the fact that Arabic coffee and humus or olives are immediately offered to the guest, as chai is offered in India,[5] as still in Ireland the kettle is immediately boiled to offer tea to the stranger or guest.

My mother took this tradition seriously: on Christmas Eve she would light a large candle and place it on the windowsill facing the street. This was 'to light the Christchild through the snow'. Despite the scepticism of her children – who tried to point out that the Christchild had been born far from our northern city of Newcastle-on-Tyne – she gently told us that welcoming the stranger on this night was welcoming Christ, who had not been made welcome in the town of his birth.

What is important is that hospitality also includes a culture of care and respect for the guest – drawing on ancient traditions. Jewish tradition remembers the injunction to welcome the stranger, 'because you were strangers in Egypt'.[6] And this tradition is still revered in Judaism. A meal setting provides a context where the guest's story is told. A listening culture is created as story evokes memory and response from those who listen, or 'hearken', as the old English word expressively says. '*Cor ad cor loquitur*' ('heart speaks to heart') was the way Cardinal Newman expressed the integrity of the mutuality of true conversation. This is a listening that may be conducive to the settling of disputes: Jean Zaru referred to the process of *sulha*, or reconciliation, that was often concluded by sharing a cup of coffee.[7] Traditions of hospitality may allow the best side of human nature to come to the fore.

One of my own earliest memories is of a meal in the street to celebrate the end of World War Two in 1945. Long trestle tables were laid in the middle of the streets, where normally cars and buses would race. Strangers sat with strangers and exchanged stories. The atmosphere was one of joy and celebration. Children normally separated by religious divides played games together. I learnt early of a connection between sharing meals and peacemaking.

Hospitality in the ministry of Jesus

The next step is to enter the Gospels' world to catch a glimpse of the integral part that sharing meals played as part of Jesus' ministry of reconciliation. Hardly a page in the Gospels is without some reference to food or not in the context of a meal. This was a ministry that recognized that people needed to be fed, their hunger and thirst recognized and responded to. More importantly, and part of the subversive agenda of the dawning kingdom, poor and marginalized people needed to be fed. Jesus stands out in appealing to a more profound hunger and thirst than the merely physical. Whereas Christianity now considers his farewell meal to be remembered as the foundation of the Eucharist (with elements of forgiveness and reconciliation flowing right through it), there are eucharistic resonances permeating his entire ministry, from picnics on the hillside or lakeside, meals taken with friends in households, moving to the great climax of the post-Resurrection meal at Emmaus for Luke, and the breakfast on the shore for John.[8] Meals also occur as celebration of forgiveness and reconciliation: in the discussion of the three stories about seeking what is lost (Luke 15), it is significant that in each parable – the Lost Sheep, the Lost Coin and the Prodigal Son – there is celebration with a meal. The conversion of Zacchaeus (Luke 19) was marked not only by restitution of debts but also by a meal of welcome and rejoicing in his house. It should not be forgotten that Jesus chose to eat with poor people, by whom meat was rarely eaten, fish was consumed more as a sauce, and usually people ate coarse brown bread or barley bread.[9] But historically, the most significant story of Jesus' hospitality to the multitudes was in his feeding of five thousand people with five loaves and two fishes.

The meal on the mountain[10]

The Mount of the Beatitudes occupies a stunning site overlooking the Sea of Galilee. Despite the fact that it is virtually impossible to imagine the lonely, deserted place where the Gospel writers describe the Feeding of the Five Thousand, given the bustling traffic of tourist coaches and steady commercial activity of tourist shops today, the atmosphere has not completely vanished. The sea still sparkles, its shores still evoke memories of breakfast on the shore after a night's fishing, and Capernaum offers today, in its ruined state, a glimpse of what a small fishing village must have resembled: the panorama from the Church of the Beatitudes still embraces the landscapes where Jesus and his followers journeyed day after day through villages and desert places.

We do not know exactly what location Luke had in mind for this miraculous picnic in a desert place. Given he had probably never been to Palestine, and that Matthew places the Sermon on a mountain, whereas Luke chooses a plain, I imagine the meal somewhere in the region of the Mount of Beatitudes – in the spirit of its teaching, mindful of the prophetic heritage this teaching has inspired.[11] And still its legacy remains vibrant. Today in Palestine the Sermon on the Plain/Mount is the enduring inspiration of Elias Chacour, the charismatic Archbishop of Galilee. As a small boy he would escape to the mountain, experiencing a strong sense of Christ's presence, and still now, at every crisis he returns to its message, hoping to find a way forward in the current political impasse. As I walk the mountain paths of this area, my mind makes links between the struggles of New Testament communities under Rome's occupation at the time of the first Christmas, and the memories of Elias Chacour as he tried to come to terms with his family's eviction from the Galilean village of Biram in 1948 and his more recent struggles and immense achievements in the village of Ibillin.[12] If, in Jerusalem, the very stones cry out, here in Galilee many different aspects of the landscape tell the story of vanished villages.

All contemporary biblical commentators see the meal story on the mountain as eucharistic in foretaste and resonance. The familiar stress on hospitality is evident: 'and he welcomed them' and 'cured those who had need of healing'.[13] As ever, a response to the bodily needs of people is integral to hospitality. This is a deserted place, and Jesus will feed them as God fed the Israelites in the desert (Exod. 16.13–18). We need to imagine the desolation of being in the wilderness as darkness comes – and being hungry, with no likelihood of sustenance. On a journey in the Rajasthan desert, as part of travelling with Wells for India, it happened that darkness arrived as our jeep was stuck in sand dunes, far from the town we were aiming for. There was no way we could move for some time. One of our group, who knew well the people of the desert, walked far into the sand dunes till she found a family, who came and offered us chai. No miracle, no bread and fishes, but the hospitality of the desert people – all the Gospel writers would have understood.

Here, this proto-eucharistic meal on the mountain alerts us to the dimension of justice, often ignored or forgotten in liturgical and sacramental circles; justice at the heart of a praxis of reconciliation. For the hunger that Jesus satisfies does not occur in a time-free bubble. Bread is always dependent on being able to harvest wheat or rye; fish stocks rely on people respecting the limits of the seas; supplies of wine need careful attention to the vineyards all the year round; and water is vulnerable to climate change as well as political factors – as Chapter 1 has already made clear. That justice has been a factor in eucharistic celebrations – but its impact weakened by the gradual clericalization of the sacraments and the spiritualizing of its meaning – has been drawn to our attention by a variety of writers, not all of them liberation theologians.[14] The fact that Christianity became the religion of the Roman Empire gradually removed from view that the first Christians – and the people of Palestine – struggled under occupation to find enough to eat. Recall the complaint in Acts of the Apostles that 'their widows were being neglected in the daily distribution' (Acts 6.1–2).

There are vital connections to be made between these struggles and the struggles of poor people across the Middle East today. Some people do have enough to eat, but many – even families living close to Manger Square in Bethlehem today – experience harsh poverty. Gaza is being brought to its knees with hunger and lack of water and medical facilities. Worse still, NGOs are refused permission to enter with humanitarian supplies as all crossings are still closed. On a global scale, 1.6 billion people have no access to clean water and 2.5 billion have no sanitation.[15] Every year, 3 million children die from dysentery – 6,000 a day from water-borne diseases such as gastro-enteritis. In fact some 80 per cent of diseases in the poor south are water-related.

These facts place Christmas hospitality on a wider canvas. Our 'Christ-mas' (the very meaning of the word Christmas) recalls that Christ was born into the world to assuage its hunger – on many levels. Remembering the meals that Jesus shared, and the blessing of the loaves and fishes on the mountain, we connect with the communities who have not even the barest means of sustenance, who are cut off from working the land to produce it and are forced into a political system where there is no equity of sharing the earth's resources. How to revitalize this remembering is part of the praxis of reconciliation; in this instance, especially with reconciliation with the earth.

I imagine the people on this hillside (or desert place) returning home, inspired by Jesus' words and satisfied by their meal, their hopes and dreams reawakened. Maybe a full moon shining over the sea helps them to find the way to their own village: some people had been healed, all had been fed, and the poor had had the good news preached to them – just as Isaiah had foretold. Was, they wondered, the promised Messiah, the child of peace, born in Bethlehem, now in their midst?

Beyond the first step of satisfying hunger, Jesus showed that hospitality is wider than the meal itself: he is generous with his time and energies – always being stopped as he journeys on the road, he makes room for the needs of yet more people. It is a hospitality that is independent of owning possessions: his welcome takes place on hills, lakesides and in the homes of other people. His hospitality is also one of paradoxical reversal, when the last shall be first and the first last. It is a hospitality of reaching across barriers, moving from his own people to a universalist outreach. Jesus is also sensitive to where hospitality is *not* offered, as in the house of Simon the Pharisee, where he contrasted the lack of welcome he experienced with the hospitality showered on him by the unnamed woman, whose generous love enabled her forgiveness (Luke 7.36–50). He would reverse this lack of welcome by welcoming his own disciples by washing their feet (John 13.1–12).

The Gospel story that links best with the Christmas feast is the Wedding Banquet (Luke 14.1–24; Matt. 22.1–10), where the invited guests have refused their invitation with excuses that Kenneth Bailey insists Middle-Eastern people would find both ludicrous and offensive.[16] In this story, which has resonances of Isaiah's great banquet on the Holy Mountain (Isa. 25.6–9),[17] Jesus is at great lengths to stretch the barriers of hospitality to include outcast and stranger, for hospitality traditions sometimes allow the usual boundaries to be transcended. Even when the lame and the blind have come, there are still places to be filled. So others are *compelled* to come. But compulsion should not be understood in a violent way. Rather, as the eleventh-century Middle-Eastern biblical scholar and polymath, Ibn-al-Tayyib wrote:

'Oblige them to come in.' This does not mean compulsion or force or persecution, but refers to the strength of the need for urgent solicitation, because those living outside the town see themselves as unworthy to enter into the places of the rich and eat banquets. Such outsiders need someone to confirm that there is indeed a welcome awaiting them there.[18]

In the Gospels' context we can understand the welcome as embracing the Gentiles, if Israel herself has refused the invitation: in a more contemporary ecclesial context it can refer to eucharistic hospitality, with an invitation to make connections with ecology and justice-making.[19] Richard Becher sets the story within the feast as a parable of the work of the Spirit drawing people together – 'making the connections':

So the Spirit of God continued hovering over the chaos of the world, singing the good news of a wonderful banquet to which everyone was invited. She swept through the streets and alleys of the towns; the fields and valleys of the country, inviting the rich and the poor, the blind and the lame, servants and masters, to follow the light that would lead them to where God was celebrating . . . So God sent the Spirit back to the city streets and country lanes to invite all who were poor to come and celebrate the good news but warned that the wealthy and powerful who had declined to come would not taste the fruits of the kingdom, found in the stable.[20]

Of all the wise people in the world, the story continues, only three from the East completed the journey – and on being told to go to the town to spread the news, no one had time to celebrate with God. Across the centuries, the Spirit still blows across the world inviting all creation to celebrate the feast.

Sharing meals and reconciliation

Primarily the Christmas feast celebrates God's generosity in the gift of Christ, the flesh-taking of the divine, the entry of divinity into the painful, inglorious yet blessed human history. However conflicted is our world, there is always reason to celebrate – maybe even more so because of the conflict. For example, Pastor Mitri Raheb, founder of the International Center of Bethlehem (ICB), confronted this dilemma in the Intifada of 1987, when there seemed little to celebrate. Christmas celebrations were cancelled in Bethlehem. 'Yet', he told his congregation in his Christmas sermon:

> God comes into the world in, through, and with this child. God himself becomes like our Palestinian refugees. He becomes one of us, one who was driven from his homeland . . . So we have not been deserted . . . God enters this world as a very small and powerless baby; but just so he overcomes this world.[21]

So celebrating the feast is affirming the powers of light and goodness over the powers of darkness. Even in the sharing of the simplest of meals, the seeds or fruits of reconciliation may be sown, as I experienced recently in Rajasthan. Our group were the guests of a village community who invited us, the visiting team of Wells for India, to an evening meal. Seated on the sand, with leaves of the neem tree as our plates, we were given simple food – but so costly for this poor community, who served us generously. Our leader, a respected Gandhian, explained our presence, giving the experience a deeper meaning:

> Yes, they are British. And, yes, Britain used to rule our country. We wanted the British to go. Gandhi himself led the 'Quit India' campaign. But now they are back – not as conquerors, but as partners. Together we will tackle the problems you have here – no water and no dignity of life.

It was a breakthrough moment and the beginning of a new relationship.

Many personal stories show the possibility of healing inherent in a meal in a diversity of settings. And in the context of meal encounters to achieve mutuality, greater understanding and pointers towards reconciliation, stories abound. One initiative – *Kedem*, the Hebrew acronym for 'Voices for Religious Reconciliation' – reveals this role. *Kedem*, an initiative of the Interreligious Coordinating Council in Israel, facilitates encounters across the three faiths of Palestine/Israel. It is indicative that some of the most fruitful encounters have taken place in Northern Ireland, with its long history of religious conflict.[22] This follows the same inspiration I experienced in Rwanda in 2004, where the Faith and Order Commission of the World Council of Churches – at whose invitation I came to Rwanda – deliberately chose a theatre of conflict for its deliberations in preparing material for the next Assembly. Ron Kronish explains the sharing of meals among the leaders of the three faiths as a particularly vital part in the process:

> The group then enjoyed its first and only Sabbath meal together. It was a moving, spiritual occasion, not only because the religious leaders were able to break bread together . . . but also because of the act of coming together in religious fellowship . . . this coming together over a simple Shabbat meal was unquestionably one of the highlights of this journey on the path to reconciliation.[23]

How these meals of fellowship can develop into the real breakthrough needed for reconciliation such as that experienced by the Norwegian villagers in the opening quotation to this chapter is our contemporary challenge.[24]

The hospitality of the Christmas feast

Having looked at traditions in the Gospels around sharing a meal in the time of Jesus, it is time to confront the issues facing us today. Candles light up darkened corners, the Christmas tree sparkles with lights, there are fragrant smells of pine logs burning, mulled wine, roasting turkey, grilling fish or vegetarian lasagne – all are familiar aspects of Christmas Day. And there are many cultural differences and preferences all over the world. Who would want to be the ghost at the feast and complain of this seasonal festivity? Would we have begrudged Bob Cratchit and his family, in the well-loved story by Charles Dickens, the first goose they had ever enjoyed?[25] The sense of blessing expressed by Tiny Tim – 'God bless us every one!' – is integral to the feast.

But there are other considerations: the first is the call to take a prophetic stance against extravagance and to practise the simplicity of our Advent lifestyle. There are many ways to do this, and to celebrate in a way that avoids waste, in harmony with environmental considerations, as well as in keeping with the spirit of festivity.

Second, the practice of Christmas hospitality is the same call as that of the Wedding Banquet in the Gospels: who is welcome in our households? Who will be guests at our tables? Christmas is a time of great loneliness for many people. It is a time of fear for families of alcoholics. Police also fear alcohol-related deaths in the festive season. Families themselves are sometimes placed in a socially impossible situation in which they are forced to be artificially festive with members with whom they do not usually speak, let alone interrelate. For others, whose relationships may have broken down, the compulsion to 'be jolly' is painful and reinforces a sense of failure and brokenness. Many families dread Christmas because poverty means that they find it difficult to pay bills, let alone join in what seems to be forced festivity and compulsive extravagance. Some parents are forced to tell their children to expect nothing as Christmas presents. In some countries the accent on Christmas is different: in the Netherlands, for example – where gifts have already been given at the feast of St Nicholas – the Christmas meal is one of nostalgia as families remember the loved ones who are no longer with them. In other countries, and countries where the established faith is that of the Orthodox Church, Christmas is celebrated on 6 January.

For homeless people, the experience of Christmas can be far from joyful. Charities such as Crisis make immense efforts to offer hospitality and a sense of caring: recently this has developed into a year-round activity, as the staff address the deep-rooted causes of homelessness, now aggravated by the economic crisis. But only a fraction of those in need can be included within these efforts.

All this challenges our notions of hospitality to look deeper into the kind of society we are. Are we in fact a hospitable society, or do notions of hospitality only include those who prosper, have good incomes and can afford to indulge in the extravaganza of spending? Nowhere are our notions of welcome and hospitality called into question more radically than by the growing numbers of refugees and asylum seekers. How do they fit into the hospitality of the Christmas feast?

The refugees of Palestine – hospitality refused?

One evening in 2008, the participants in the seventh Sabeel International Conference were guests of the Dheishe refugee camp in Bethlehem. Many of the older hosts were former refugees from *al-Nakba* ('the catastrophe') of 1948. The memory of that dispossession, and the stories of the flight to Bethlehem, are still alive and poignant. On the walls of the camp are painted murals – large keys are everywhere: these are door keys, the symbol of the longing to return home. One group was welcomed to the home of a grandmother, who told me her story:

The Grandmother's Tale

The child Jesus became a refugee from Bethlehem.
But now, the town itself is full of refugees,
these camps now 'home' to thousands who have fled,
driven out at gunpoint by Israeli soldiers,
now 60 years since the taking of their land.
This grandmother tells her story.
She too took the road to Bethlehem those days,
forced from her house – she took the key!
A young girl then, stumbling painfully – what was the hurry?

102

From Deir Aban, beloved home.
Mothers, fathers, frightened children,
all forced to take the road to Bethlehem.
And, like Mary of the ancient story,
one pregnant mother forced to run along the road,
in terror brings forth her child –
Oh no! that's too dignified a phrase!
The baby drops to the earth, blood-covered,
and the anguished mother is forced to stumble on,
abandoning the child . . .
But maybe there's an angel presence as of old,
for someone finds the child and carries him to Bethlehem,
to his mother, half-crazed with sorrow.
Where still his family lives.
Where still the grandmother lives.
Those early tents have changed to houses,
Yet still she sleeps, key under pillow:
This her dream – the right to return!

When Joseph took the road to Bethlehem,
with pregnant Mary,
I think his kinsfolk would have welcomed him,
in humble homes, where animals shared space with people,
then Bethlehem still hoped and longed
for the child to usher in the longed-for peace.
Two thousand years have passed –
Unchanged the dream.[26]

This story made a great impact on all the listeners. It was even more amazing to go out into the street and meet the 'baby' of 60 years ago, now a soldier, alive and well. As we feasted with our hosts – on chicken and rice – the air was alive with memories of the past and the pain of the present. Small wonder that at Christmas, charities focus on the situation of refugees and see this as a challenge to the hospitality of our society and the real meaning of Christmas.

Who are the Palestinian refugees?

The number of Palestinian refugees varies depending on the source consulted. For 1948–9 refugees, for example, the Israeli government suggests a number as low as 520,000, as opposed to 850,000 by their Palestine counterparts. UNRWA (United Nations Relief and Works Agency for Palestine Refugees in the Near East) cites 726,000 people.[27] UNRWA provides facilities in 59 recognized refugee camps in Jordan, Lebanon, Syria, the West Bank and the Gaza Strip. It also provided relief to displaced persons inside the State of Israel following the 1948 conflict until the Israeli government took over responsibility for them in 1952. For a camp to be recognized by UNRWA, there must be an agreement between the host government and UNRWA governing the use of the camp. UNRWA does not itself run any camps, has no police powers or administrative role, but simply provides services to the camp. Refugee camps, which developed from tented cities to rows of concrete blockhouses to urban ghettos indistinguishable from their surroundings, house around one third of all registered Palestinian refugees.

UNRWA's services are available to all those living in its area of operations who meet this definition, who are registered with the agency and who need assistance. Its definition of a refugee also covers the descendants of persons who became refugees in 1948. The number of registered Palestinian refugees has subsequently grown from 914,000 in 1950 to more than 4.3 million in 2005.[28]

But, of course, the Palestinian situation must be placed within a wider context of why people choose to migrate and what are the responsibilities of the international community. There are many different types of migration, and different causes. In India, as in many countries, there has been an ancient practice of seasonal migration of herders and pastoral people seeking water and fodder for their flocks. Shepherds will migrate as much as 1,000 miles, returning in time for the monsoon – a time-honoured strategy for survival. But in the last 50 years, endemic rural poverty has been worsened by poor development policies and India's neglect of infrastructure in the effort to become a great player in the world of global capitalism.

More than 60 per cent of Indians live in villages, often remote and with difficult access to water sources and medical care. About a third (300–350 million) of all Indians live below the UN poverty level. If we look closely at causes, it is not only economic policies and water shortage aggravated by cycles of drought and flood, but the caste system that keeps Dalit people – and there are 200 million Dalits in India – locked into degradation and ineluctable poverty. One cause of migration hardly ever referred to is the attempt to escape such discrimination: it is not often realized, for example, that there are over 200,000 Dalits living in Britain.

Asia is home to 87 per cent of the world's known 400 million small farmers, all especially vulnerable to climate change as they rely on regular and reliable rainfall. So in this one continent there are complex reasons for migration: a destabilization through economic poverty caused by unjust economic structures of global capitalism benefiting only the rich few, internally through caste discrimination and neglect of the rural areas, and today, by a recession caused by the richest countries. If we then factor in climate change, the result is to affect and deepen all these points.

A last point about India is to remember that what still haunts this country is what is called 'the wounded history of India'. This is the partition of 1947, the tragic memory of a country split artificially in the creation of Pakistan, with the terrible slaughter on both sides, the displacement and permanent division of families and enduring hostilities it entailed. It is a tragic appeal to the need for reconciliation on an immense scale. Indians speak of it today as a wound worse than colonialism. But the image that continues to haunt many people concerned about justice and peace is people living in slums or on pavements in India's great cities. (More people are aware now because of the recent film *Slumdog Millionaire*.) This is another example of internal migration because of the lack of sustainable life in villages. In great civilizations, flight to the cities has happened everywhere village sustainability has been neglected.

Another context raises another reason for migration: that of fleeing from conflict. Five years ago (2004) I went to Rwanda with a small group from the World Council of Churches: the focus was meant to be the environment, and the organizers had deliberately chosen to approach this focus from a context of violence.[29] What happened was that our eyes were opened not only to the horror of the genocide of 1994 (nearly one million Tutsis were massacred), but also to the ongoing conflicts of the Great Lakes area of Africa. We began to understand how the poisonous genocidal aftermath of a colonial era has impacted, and continues to impact on this region, generating many war refugees from Rwanda, Burundi and especially the Democratic Republic of the Congo. In the case of Rwanda, the colonizing countries had been Belgium and Germany, which had privileged Tutsi over Hutu, arousing bitter enmity between two groups who, over a period of hundreds of years, had been able to coexist relatively peacefully.

These ongoing conflicts in Africa and the Middle East – Iraq, Iran, Palestine and now Afghanistan/Pakistan – all have implications for the refugees in the cities of Europe and North America. They also raise questions about our own ongoing responsibility both for the causes of their leaving their homes as well as the *kinds of welcoming communities* we create here to receive them. Refugees from climate change are the most significant growing category of people on the move. Hardly a day passes without a report of another disaster in the poor Global South (all recent articles declare that 99 per cent of climate refugees come from there), and once more people are on the move. When water and agriculture fail, life is unsustainable for both people and animals. People take to the oceans in fragile craft (and ever since the Vietnamese boat people we have seen the tragedies that can then occur), fleeing not only the torture of brutal regimes but also lands that cannot, for a complex set of reasons, nourish them any more. As global warming seems set to worsen, if we cannot commit ourselves to effective action, we will witness growing numbers of 'environmental refugees'. And in the end, there will be nowhere for any of us to go.

This discussion cannot end without a mention of the plight of asylum seekers. Despite the efforts of the Independent Asylum Commission to improve the legal status of Asylum Seekers,[30] the work of groups like London Citizens and local activist voluntary groups, and the contribution of active church groups backed by church leadership,[31] the situation is acute. Women and children are suffering particularly severely: these are innocent victims, effectively imprisoned. Parents fear lasting psychological damage to their children. As the wider situation of war in places like Afghanistan/Pakistan deteriorates, cases of asylum will escalate. Many more people will come with stories of torture.

This calls for us to factor in to all our networking for justice and peace, across the faiths and beyond, an interconnectedness of all justice and peace issues, and to foster a lifestyle that means hospitality for all God's creation and creatures. Can the Christmas feast act as a wakeup call to the severity of the challenge to us to become a more welcoming society? How do the Christmas traditions of hospitality help with a level of severe suffering and need?

First of all, can the Bible help? The Old Testament is no stranger to issues of exile, fleeing, wandering and the need to welcome the stranger, as we have seen. The ministry of Jesus highlights the current Middle-Eastern tradition of hospitality. Second, Christianity has a long tradition of offering hospitality and welcome to poor and sick people through the many religious orders and their more recent offspring, lay orders and lay-inspired communities such as L'Arche and Sant'Egidio in Rome – which itself began by working with groups of refugees.

Third, Christians all have a commitment to justice with many strands: there is a long tradition of justice encyclicals in the Roman Catholic Church that perhaps suffer from being inadequately communicated; there is a commitment to meeting people's basic human needs and recognizing the full humanity of all women and men, to making the law work for justice,[32] and there is the work of the aid agencies over the last 40 years, to developing a prophetic spirituality of justice that inspires a lifestyle enabling us to look beyond narrow boundaries and act globally for justice, to take risks beyond the familiar and comfortable. It is a spirituality that challenges us to move beyond stereotypes and probe behind what passes for truth in the public discourse.

Here, as always, the Holy Spirit, who was invoked in the I–Thou phenomenon of Annunciation (see Chapter 2), inspires us here to work for truth and integrity, embodying in a just way the reality that every human being is created in God's image. Just as in the early days of development education, development agencies had to challenge false myths on poverty, development and racism, now, in this new phase of working for social justice, we have to challenge myths and specious arguments around asylum, migration and refugees – such as accusing people of only coming for the benefit system, or agreeing to the principle that torture works and is an acceptable means to an end, with merely temporary effects.

The task seems enormous and daunting. But in it we are assisted by a deep conviction that the God of justice is on our side. No more do we rely, if ever we did, on the distant transcendent 'God in the sky' – hardly an inspiring image. No: God is vulnerable, and with us in the search for justice and wellbeing for some of her most beloved creatures, now vulnerable. Christmas is the moment of that divine vulnerability breaking through into human and non-human earthly life. Although the Christ story will move on from the birth event to offer social redemption through the gift of life and promise of eternal life, already at Christmas this is a gift that challenges the expensive excessive giving of society – with the promise of joy and hope. This promise comes with the practice of simplicity and the opening of our doors to those who flee in fear from situations for which we may be partly responsible.

Thomas Merton, a Trappist monk and peace activist, captures this sense of vulnerability of God to the human tragedies of our day, and the divine longing to participate in love. His words here capture the message of Christmas; the vulnerable God walks with her children:

> The shadows fall. The stars appear. The birds begin to sleep. Night embraces the silent half of the earth. A vagrant, a destitute wanderer with dusty feet, finds his way down a new road. A homeless God, lost in the night, without papers, without identification, without even a number, a frail expendable exile lies down in desolation under the sweet stars of the world and entrusts Himself [Herself] to sleep.[33]

This gift of a vulnerable God is what we celebrate at Christmas. And each of us, in our own contexts and resources, will find the strength and means to find a way to a true generosity of giving. The Christmas stars will shine brighter this year, as people reach out through practising a simpler, more meaningful giving to one which embraces other regions of the world, to a giving that breaks down the barriers of an inhospitable society and at the same time is sowing the seeds of peace and reconciliation. That is the radiance of the Christian midnight, well captured by Nativity scenes both in traditional art and some more recent examples from many cultures across the world. It is the radiance of the meal of reconciliation with which this chapter began, the radiance that is the promise of every meal of goodwill, however simple. This message of Christmas hospitality is well expressed by a Lebanese song, '*Leilat al-Milad*' ('Night of the Birth'):[34]

Verses:
When we offer a drink to a thirsty person, then we are in
    Christmas
When we clothe a naked person with a cloak or dress of love,
    then we are in Christmas
When we wipe out tears from the eyes of those who weep, then
    we are in Christmas
When we warm up or put a mattress for somebody and the
    hearts are filled with hope, then we are in Christmas

When I kiss my companion or friend without cheating, then
    I am in Christmas
When the spirit of revenge dies out in me, then I will be in
    Christmas
When my heart has no more grudge, then I will be in Christmas
When my soul melts in God's being, then I will be in Christmas

Refrain:
During Christmas night no more hate
During Christmas night the soil flourishes
During Christmas night war is buried
During Christmas night love grows

Epilogue: Epiphany – the journey carries on

An old Russian legend tells of one icy winter's night, when the snow lay deep and the wind howled around the wooden hut of an old woman, a Baboushka, or grandmother. As she huddled over the leaping flames of her fire of blazing pine logs, she heard a faint noise of someone approaching, and then a knock on the door. To her amazement, standing in the snow were three Wise Men, dressed in splendid fashion and carrying precious caskets of gold, encrusted with jewels – and she smelt the fragrances of frankincense and myrrh. They told her that they were on their way to Bethlehem to seek the Prince of Peace, and all three urged her to come with them and offer her gift too. But the night was too cold and the snow was too deep, and poor Baboushka felt her age severely. Bethlehem was too far away and, sadly, she bade them continue without her. But as the night took its course, her sadness gave way to joy, as she thought that there was indeed something she could do and give. Yes, the newborn child was a prince, but he was also a baby. She knew what babies liked, and filled her basket with toys and balls and bright tinsel. But to her dismay the traces of the Wise Men were lost in the snow and, though she wandered from village to village, Baboushka never found the Prince of Peace. But every year at Christmas time Baboushka goes from village to village when the evening lamps are lit, and brings her simple gifts to every house where there is a baby or a small child.[1]

A legend this may be, but it is one that evokes the continuing meaning of the Epiphany story – its journey, its quest and its revelation – told to us only by Matthew's Gospel (1.18—2.23). In this sense of continuing quest for peace and reconciliation, Epiphany offers a fitting conclusion. First, we look at its traditional meaning for Western and Eastern Christians, and then at its potential for the wider journey explored here.

A cluster of meanings has evolved around the story of the three Wise Men/Magi/Kings, known traditionally – but not biblically – as Melchior, Caspar and Balthasar. They are supposed to have journeyed from Persia: the word *magoi* in this context means 'wise men' from the East. The kernel of the story is that the coming of the Christchild is not only a gift for the House of Israel but also for the wider world, biblically speaking – the Gentiles. This is Christmas day for the Gentiles, according to Western Christianity, and of special importance for Eastern Christianity too. Yet again the prophet Isaiah is drawn upon liturgically as a biblical foretelling of this wider significance of Christmas:

> Arise, shine, for your light has come, and the glory of the LORD has risen upon you. For behold, darkness shall cover the earth, and thick darkness the peoples . . . A multitude of camels shall cover you, the young camels of Midian and Ephah; all those from Sheba shall come. They shall bring gold and frankincense, and shall bring good news, the praises of the LORD.[2] (Isa. 60.1–2, 6)

A major difference between East and West is precisely what this feast commemorates. For Western Christians, the feast primarily celebrates the coming of the three Wise Men, while Eastern Churches celebrate the Baptism of Christ in the Jordan. But in both traditions the essence of the feast is similar: the manifestation of Christ to the world (whether as an infant, or in the River Jordan in a Trinitarian context), together with the whole mystery of the incarnation – and therein lie disagreements and tensions vis-à-vis Judaism and Islam, which cannot accept the Christian claim that Jesus is the Son of God.

In the West, by the year 534 AD, the Church had separated the celebration of the Nativity of Christ as the feast of Christmas, and set its date as 25 December.[3] So 6 January then became the feast of the commemoration of the coming of the Magi. But the Eastern Church continued to celebrate 6 January as a composite feast of the Baptism of Jesus. Later, it adopted 25 December to commemorate both Jesus' birth and the coming of the Magi, but kept 6 January as a commemoration of the Baptism. This meant the shining forth and revelation of Jesus Christ as the Messiah and Second Person of the Trinity at the time of his baptism.[4] It is also celebrated because, according to tradition, the baptism of Jesus in the River Jordan by John marked one of only two occasions when all three Persons of the Trinity manifested themselves simultaneously to humanity: God as Father by speaking through the clouds; God as Son being baptized in the river; God as Holy Spirit in the shape of a dove descending from heaven (the other occasion was the Transfiguration on Mount Tabor). Thus the feast of Epiphany is considered by the Eastern Church to be a manifestation, a revelation of the Holy Trinity.[5]

Revelation and epiphanies of connection

Here I want to link with a more literary meaning of 'epiphany' as a moment of inspiration and revelation. This is in order to draw Epiphany into the journey to peace and reconciliation today. This idea of epiphany depends on the novelist James Joyce who, in his novel, *A Portrait of the Artist as a Young Man*,[6] referred to those times in his life when something became manifest as a deep realization: he would then attempt to write this *epiphanic* realization in a fragment. Joyce also used epiphany as a literary device within each short story of his collection, *Dubliners*,[7] as his protagonists came to sudden recognitions that changed their views of themselves or their social condition, often sparking reversals or changes of heart. More related to the meaning I am exploring – an *epiphany of connection* (referred to in Chapter 2 in relation to annunciation in its aspect of mutuality) – is the way the Jewish philosopher Emmanuel Levinas understood epiphany, namely as a manifestation of the divine as seen in the face of the other. In the face of the other, the infinite is glimpsed. This has deep ethical implications: 'The other becomes my neighbour precisely through the way the face summons me, calls for me, begs for me, and in so doing recalls my responsibility, and calls me into question.'[8]

This draws us nearer to what I evoke: *epiphanies of connection* – similar to John Taylor's *annunciations* as I–Thou encounters[9] – offer potential to break through barriers of hostility. Levinas introduces the notion of our responsibility to the other through the bare encounter with the other's face – *especially where the other is encountered as a hostile other*. Responding to the relational encounter can lead to mutual understanding and eventually to reconciliation. Epiphany can thus act as a beckoning star drawing us further towards making valuable connections for peace.

But how can this work practically, given the barriers that now prevent mutual understanding? Can celebrating Christmas/Epiphany offer this kind of possibility? I suggest that if celebrating Christmas asked us to focus on offering hospitality as a society, in changing attitudes to homelessness, refugees and asylum seekers, Epiphany, because of its wider outreach, offers the chance to overcome other barriers – such as between faiths, in our common search for peace.

Christmas/Epiphany – invitation for a Muslim–Jewish–Christian encounter?[10]

For Islam, celebrating Christmas does not offer much attraction. The two Islamic feasts are Eid-el Adhha (the feast of the sacrifice) and Eid-el Fitr (the feast of ending the fast of the month of Ramadan). Although in Western countries some Muslims may put up Christmas trees, and see no harm in celebrating the Prophet Jesus' birthday, this does not generally happen in predominantly Islamic lands. Christmas is seen as a feast of excess, an occasion for eating extravagantly and drinking to excess – rather like the pagan winter feast with which the origins of Christmas are linked. Yet the Qur'an actually relates the story of the birth of Christ, although it is given a very different meaning.[11] The Virgin Mary is told by an angel that she will give birth to a 'pure' son, 'as a sign unto men and a mercy from Us'. She withdraws to a desert place, alone, and gives birth to the baby under a palm tree. When she returns with the baby to her people, they presume Mary has been unfaithful, but the infant Jesus speaks up from his cradle in her defence, telling them that he is a prophet. The passage concludes with a denunciation of the doctrine of the Incarnation – but it is interpreted in polytheistic terms, whereas Christians in reality do not believe in three gods. Muslims cannot celebrate Christmas because of this misinterpretation of the Incarnation. Yet Palestinian educators see that building a common understanding between Muslims and Christians is important. In Bethlehem, for example:

The textbooks of the Palestinian authority pay attention to Jesus and Mary, Bethlehem and Christmas, and regularly school classes of Moslem students visit the Church of Nativity on a fieldtrip (which is not only a religious but also a national symbol for Palestinians).[12]

Similar difficulties haunt Jewish–Christian relations around Christmas. It is puzzling and problematic, says Rabbi Dan Cohn-Sherbok:

As a little boy growing up in the leafy suburbs of Denver, I remember being an angel in a nativity play in my elementary school. A rather odd role for a Jewish six year old. But no one seemed to mind. At home we opened Christmas presents on Christmas day. But no tree was allowed. In pulpits rabbis fulminated against those congregants who had Christmas trees in their living rooms. Yet no mention was made about exchanging gifts. It was all most perplexing. The Rabbi's ban on Christmas trees caused my mother frustration and a degree of distress. As an artist, she wanted to decorate a Christmas tree with home-made objects. But it was not to be. Instead we had a rather pathetic Hanukkah bush. I recall being taken in my parents' car to look at all the houses in Denver displaying Christmas lights outside. My mother sighed as we drove through the streets of Denver. She would have liked to decorate our house, too. But this was a major taboo.[13]

Not only the trappings of Christmas but its message were off-limits – to Dan Cohn-Sherbok it seemed rather fanciful.

But there are important reasons for attempting a closer understanding at this moment. The first is that Christmas, as we have been noting, whatever its religious origins and aspirations, is now celebrated with commercialist excess in the form of presents, food and drink – even decadence. There are issues here of lost values and of environmental damage that concern all faiths – and as already noted, this 'decadence' is deeply offensive to Muslims.

The second reason is more crucial: Christmas – beneath the tinsel – is actually about peace. Yet the lack of peace is what haunts our world, and the crucible of sorrow is in the Middle East and the still-festering wounds of Iraq, as well as complex unfolding tragedies in Afghanistan. Christianity and Judaism both play roles in the Middle East. Could closer understandings of the Christmas and Epiphany message offer inspiration at this juncture?

Following Levinas' injunction to take responsibility for the face of the other means taking seriously what Jews bring to Christmas, namely:

> a fearful legacy of 20 centuries of suffering and murder. Easter, of course, is worse . . . through the history of Jewish–Christian encounter Jews have been vilified for Jesus' death . . . it is not easy for Jews to set aside this terrible history of persecution in the quest to find spiritual meaning in the celebration of Jesus' birth.[14]

No one underestimates the difficulty: the challenge is to begin a mutual journey to find meaning in the Christmas story. Beyond the extravagance of a commercialized Christmas season there is, as this book has explored, the promise of peace in our troubled and troubling world.

Dan Cohn-Sherbok in his turn highlights the Middle East as a focus for concern:

> At the end of the 19th century Zionists argued that the only solution to the problem of Jew hatred would be for Jews to have a state of their own in their native homeland. But this was not to be. Today Jews everywhere are despised by the Arab world. Can the nativity scene somehow serve as a bridge between Jews and Arabs in the Holy Land?[15]

The legacy of persecution of Jews, especially by Christians, and especially at Easter, is part of taking responsibility for the other, referred to by Levinas. And this is especially so at a time when neo-Nazism is rearing its ugly head and Holocaust denial has become popular, albeit only among a small minority. Yet there is still hope that we are in a new phase, that Christmas offers a chance to move forward to some shared future, that wrongs of the past need not be repeated. The words of Maya Angelou, at the inauguration of President Clinton, express this well:

> History, despite its wrenching pain,
> Cannot be unlived, but if faced
> With courage, need not be lived again.[16]

Yet this cannot happen without true conversion of heart on the part of Christians and some sharing of the vision of the biblical peaceable kingdom. This sharing can unite the Jewish and Christian faiths through the inspiration of *tikkun olam*, a Hebrew phrase meaning 'the healing of the world', a vision that stretches beyond sectarian divides. And although the birth of Jesus at Christmas is not mentioned by the earliest Gospel writer, Mark, he begins his writing precisely by a call to proclaim the good news – 'the kingdom of God is at hand!' (Mark 1.15). Matthew and Luke project back into seeing this vision of a peaceful and just kingdom prophetically glimpsed in the child's wonder-birth. Centuries of prophetic tradition pick up on this strand of Christmas that transcends denominational barriers: it is a time for generosity for all, for true giving – to the homeless, refugees, to victims of environmental disaster.

In this way Jews and Christians can move beyond the tragedy of past Jewish–Christian relations. Over the last 100 years, a range of Jewish thinkers have encouraged their fellow Jews to look at Jesus in a new way. Even if Jews cannot accept the doctrine of Jesus' Messiahship, nor the doctrine of the Incarnation, it is still possible, as Dan Cohn-Sherbok suggests, that Jews could stand before the crib alongside their Christian brothers and sisters and wonder at Jesus' prophetic ministry. This witnesses to the strong Jewish belief that Jesus was firmly in the line of the prophets of ancient Israel. Christians, of course, need to keep in mind that Jesus was a Jew, albeit a reforming one, and remained a faithful Jew until his death. What is more, as we have been constantly appreciating, the whole of the Christmas story and events that led up to it, especially the foretelling, birth and mission of John the Baptist, are permeated with the inspiration of Isaiah, a Jewish prophet. The Midnight Mass of Christmas is redolent with the imagery of darkness to light, 'the people who walked in darkness have seen a great light' at the birth of this 'Prince of Peace', the 'Wonderful Counsellor' (Isa. 9.2, 6). In the liturgical Christian season, the Advent journey looks forward to a vision of redeemed creation, creation reconciled and made whole, and this is the shared hope of Jews and Christians, namely, the peaceable kingdom.

Within this stance, Jesus' attack on the scribes and Pharisees can be seen not as a rejection of Torah but as a prophetic renunciation of corruption. But there is more: placing himself in the line of the prophets, Jesus called the people back to the true worship of God. His words and actions testify to his dedication to compassion and loving kindness. In the case of those most sorely in need (within the theme of this book, the victims of conflict), he was able to reach out in love and compassion. Is this the Christmas message that can bind us together to create a better world despite the differences that divide us? But there is a danger that this sentiment remains at the level of generalities. How can it offer any concrete hope for, especially, a way out of deadlocked conflict in the Middle East, with the realities of the 'little town of Bethlehem' today, with which Chapter 3 began? Dan Cohn-Sherbok feels strongly that compassion for the Palestinians should not blind us to the fact that:

> For nearly four thousand years the Jewish people have been subject to persecution and murder. Your experiences in Bethlehem should not blind you to this fact. We, too, have been victims. We are separated from the Palestinian people by our aims. But we are united with them in suffering. In different ways our two peoples have been wounded, and we have wounded one another. The question is whether there can be healing in the Christian message. Can Jesus' call for a peaceable Kingdom speak to Jews and Arabs in the Holy Land?[17]

Certainly, nothing is gained by refusing to see the total picture. Opposing the policies of the Zionist government is not falling back into the old anti-Semitism. As one Jewish writer whose consciousness has changed with regard to the Israeli–Palestinian conflict put it: 'The Rabbis who will not engage . . . in an honest discussion about Israel and Palestine are not friends of Israel. We Jews are in spiritual peril and Israel itself is in great danger.'[18]

Nor should Christian shared responsibility for the choice of Palestine as the Jewish homeland be ignored. It was Lord Shaftesbury, after all, who first pronounced the influential sentence, 'A land without a people, for a people without a land'. The struggle for peace in the Middle East is multi-faceted, and religion will only be able to play a limited part. Our question here remains: What role can celebrating the Christmas feast play in this struggle?

The first point about this is to recall that, yes, this is a Christian feast and that Christians in Israel and Palestine now feel themselves a beleaguered group, the 'Forgotten Faithful' in fact.[19] Every day their numbers are dropping as huge numbers go into exile because of present conditions. They suffer too because the world does not recognize that they have kept the faith since the earliest days of the founding of Christianity, and sees the Middle-Eastern conflict as solely between Jew and Muslim. Celebrating Christmas is about affirming their identity and showing solidarity.

But, second, what Christmas can offer to our shared faith communities is its focus on a vulnerable child, threatened with murder and then becoming a refugee – a strong motif of Matthew's narrative. There are now hundreds of vulnerable children across our faith divides, and insufficient focus on what the conflict does to them. A recent report from Save the Children points out that:

> the link between climate change and child survival struggles to command public and political attention. It is vital that governments and the public understand what is at stake. Tackling the issues young children face as a result of climate change must be made a priority. Today, most child deaths occur in the world's poorest countries and communities. Children are dying from a small number of preventable and treatable diseases and conditions, including diarrhoea, malaria and malnutrition. An estimated third of the entire global childhood disease burden is attributable to changeable factors in food, soil, water and air.[20]

Third, Christmas is a time of hospitality and giving: our faiths offer resources to avoid excessive extravagance. 'Offer your heart to the infant king', says one loved carol.[21] Could this become a time of offering, of giving, of forgiveness across our faith communities? This child will grow up and offer a message of peace and non-violence that rings through the centuries. This is truly something to be shared at Christmas. The Christmas message recalls Jews as well as Muslims and Christians in the Holy Land to a vision that all can share. In different ways and at various times in their history, all three faith groups have felt victimized. The child Jesus who is adored at birth became, as an adult, a first-century prophet calling his followers to a vision of the messianic kingdom as depicted by Isaiah:

> It shall come to pass in the latter days that the mountain of the house of the LORD shall be established as the highest of the mountains, and shall be raised above the hills; and all the nations shall flow into it . . . He shall judge between the nations, and shall decide disputes for many

peoples; and they shall beat their swords into ploughshares and their spears into pruning hooks; nation shall not lift up sword against nation, neither shall they learn war any more. (Isa. 2.2–4)

Of course Jews cannot view Jesus as the long-awaited Redeemer. But his inspirational vision of peace is a central feature of the Jewish as well as Christian heritage. And it is this picture of peace that can inspire us, Jews, Christians and Muslims alike. It requires a change of heart and the willingness for all of us to forgive our enemies. Such unconditional forgiveness is not solely a Christian ideal – repeatedly rabbinic sages stressed the importance of forgiving one's enemies. As the Talmud states: 'Whoever takes vengeance or bears a grudge acts like one who, having cut one hand while handling a knife, avenges himself by stabbing the other hand.'[22]

So even if Jews cannot accept the Christology of the Christmas story, nonetheless, Christmas can inspire us all to seek God's peace on earth – on earth as it is in heaven. Even though Jews cannot accept Jesus as Messiah, perhaps Christmas encourages the possibility of a shared hope and belief in a messianic consciousness that is the willingness to work for transformation. What is more, the symbolism of the birth of this child is that the initiative of generosity and love is divine, and on this initiative rests the possibility of mutual forgiveness.

If God's economy is a gift economy, is the invitation of this feast for Jews, Christians and Muslims to transcend the realities of hate and revenge, to embrace the true gift of Christmas as forgiving love, and so bring us to the threshold of the dawning of the peaceable kingdom of reconciliation?

And thus, at the end of the feast, when the tree returns to the garden to grow quietly until the following year,[23] the true work of Christmas can begin. As Howard Thurman wrote:

> When the song of the angels is stilled,
> When the star in the sky is gone,
> When the kings and princes are home,
> When the shepherds are back with their flock,
> The work of Christmas begins:
>   To find the lost,
>   To heal the broken,

> To feed the hungry,
> To release the prisoner,
> To rebuild the nations,
> To bring peace among brothers,
> To make music in the heart.[24]

And as Auden's shepherds put it, when transformed by their visit to the newborn child of peace, in words that call out to us through the ages: 'O here and now our endless journey starts.'[25]

Appendix 1
'Broken Town'

Oh broken town of Bethlehem
Your people long for peace,
But curfews, raids and closure barricades
Have brought them to their knees.
Yet still they strive for justice
And still they make their stand
Their hopes and fears still echo down the years
Come, heal this holy land.

Oh holy child of Bethlehem,
A royal refugee,
Your place of birth is now a hell on earth
Through our complicity.
The innocents still suffer,
Their backs against the wall.
We see the curse, the violence and worse
And choose to ignore it all.

Oh holy streets of Bethlehem
Deserted and destroyed
The frightened faces fill the sacred places
Pilgrims once enjoyed.
Yet in the midst of darkness
A hopeful beacon shines:
The future lies in humble sacrifice
And not in guns and mines.

Oh holy star of Bethlehem
Help us to watch and pray.
With love and light illuminate the night
Reveal the Kingdom's day.
Lord, dare us to be angels

Your awesome truth to tell.
It must be heard:
You are the final word,
Our Lord, Emmanuel.

'Broken Town': lyrics by Martin John Nicholls from his album
Beyond Belief. © Daybreak Music Ltd. All rights reserved.
Used with permission. Dedicated to Nader Abu Amsha
and the staff of East Jerusalem YMCA, Beit Sahour

Appendix 2
Suggestions for alternative giving

———•◦•———

Suggestions from NGOs

These are gifts such as tools, educational materials, trees, goats, orchards and so on, which are sent to the NGO for their development projects. The recipient receives an attractive certificate or card.

- Oxfam Unwrapped – http://www.oxfam.org.uk/shop/oxfam-unwrapped
- Christian Aid: Present Aid – http://www.presentaid.org
- Tear Fund – http://resources.tearfund.org
- Cafod – http://cafod.force.com/worldgifts/wg_home
- Wells for India – http://www.wellsforindia.org

Gifts to help the Palestinian economy

- Zaytoun Olive Oil – http://www.traidcraft.co.uk
- Palestinian and other International Crafts – http://www.merian-derwent.org.uk
- Sunbula, a fair trade organization based in Jerusalem – http://www.sunbula.org
- Hadeel, crafts from the West Bank, Gaza and Lebanon – http://www.hadeel.org
- Taybeh: candles, crafts and 'peace lamps' – http://www.taybeh.info/en/index.php
- International Center of Bethlehem pottery, embroidery, glassware, jewellery, books – http://www.annadwa.org/cave/giftshop.htm

Notes

Introduction: the Advent journey

1 Mary Robinson, cited in Fergus Finlay, *Mary Robinson: A President with a Purpose* (Dublin: O'Brien Press, 1990), p. 156. See also Mary Grey, *To Rwanda and Back: Liberation, Spirituality and Reconciliation* (London: Darton, Longman & Todd, 2007), pp. 12–13.

2 It used to be thought that Luke was written as late as 80 AD. More recently the possible date has been put at as early as 50–60 AD, that is, before the fall of Jerusalem, the time usually ascribed to the writing of the Gospel of Mark. See Tom Wright, *Luke for Everyone* (London: SPCK, 2001), pp. 2–3. John is usually thought to be the last-written Gospel – some time before 100 AD but after the destruction of Jerusalem and the Diaspora.

3 Matthew and Luke also stress the persecution and time of tribulation, without the consoling promise that Matthew offers.

4 Zionism – the chosen philosophy of the current Israeli government, which undergirds and inspires its politics – has both Christian and Jewish antecedents, as this book describes. Its principal tenet is that the Jewish people have a divinely ordained right to the land of Israel.

5 The Sabeel Ecumenical Liberation Theology Center, Jerusalem. 'Sabeel' means the 'way' or the 'wellspring'. It is an international organization, working for peace in Palestine and Israel, especially among Christians. It is based in Jerusalem, with associated Friends around the world. See <http://www.sabeel.org/index.php>.

6 Naim Ateek, 'Historical Factors that have affected Palestinian Christians', in Naim Ateek, Cedar Duaybis and Maurine Tobin (eds), *The Forgotten Faithful: A Window into the Life and Witness of Christians in the Holy Land* (Jerusalem: Sabeel Ecumenical Liberation Theology Center, 2007), p. 69.

7 Ateek, 'Historical Factors'.

8 The story is told by Toine van Teeffelen on the website connected with the Arab Education Institute (AEI), <http://www.palestine-family.net>.

9 Yet it is disputed that since Crusaders had free access to the Church of

the Holy Sepulchre in the eleventh and twelfth centuries, the keys must still have been with the Byzantine clergy of Jerusalem and not with local Muslim families.

10 See Betty Jane Bailey and J. Martin Bailey, *Who are the Christians in the Middle East?* (Grand Rapids, MI: Eerdmans, 2003), p. 25.

11 Jean Zaru, *Occupied with Nonviolence: A Palestinian Woman Speaks* (Minneapolis, MN: Augsburg Fortress, 2008).

12 Sami Awad, unpublished lecture to the Vanishing Palestine Conference, organized by the Amos Trust, All Hallows on the Wall Church, London, 22 September 2008.

13 Here I follow Michael Prior, 'The Holy Land, Zion and the Challenge to the Church', in Michael Prior CM, *A Living Stone: Selected Essays and Addresses*, ed. Duncan Macpherson (London: Living Stones of the Holy Land Trust and Melisende, 2006), p. 249.

14 A contemporary authority on Christian Zionism is Stephen Sizer – see his *Christian Zionism: Road-Map to Armageddon?* (Leicester: InterVarsity Press, 2004) and *Zion's Christian Soldiers: The Bible, Israel and the Church* (Nottingham: InterVarsity Press, 2007).

15 The fervour that this idea aroused can be glimpsed in George Eliot's novel, *Daniel Deronda* (London: Penguin, 1974). Written in the middle of the nineteenth century, the novel's climax describes how the hero, Daniel, discovering his Jewish origins, and in love with the young Jewess Mirah, sets sail for Israel in full hope of being part of its restoration and rebuilding for the Jewish people.

16 This text is displayed in the permanent exhibition of the Jewish Museum, Vienna, which I visited in September 2008.

17 Theodor Herzl, *Der Judenstaat: Versuch einer Modernen Lösung der Juden-frage* (Leipzig and Vienna: Breitenstein, 1896). Herzl's book is translated as *The Jewish State* (New York: Dover, 1988).

18 Michael Prior, 'Reading the Bible with the Eyes of the Canaanites – in Homage to Edward Said', in Prior, *A Living Stone*, p. 277.

19 Michael Prior, 'A Land Flowing with Milk, Honey and People', in Prior, *A Living Stone*, p. 173; emphasis added.

20 Prior, 'Land Flowing with Milk', p. 173.

21 Lord Balfour – Arthur James Balfour, a former Prime Minister – was part of the War Cabinet and Foreign Secretary. The Balfour Declaration refers to the decision of the British government in 1917 to give its blessing to the movement to grant the Jews a homeland in Palestine.

22 'William Blackstone, Defender of the Jews', at <http://jerusalemprayerteam.org/pdf/022505.pdf>.

23 Naim Ateek, unpublished lecture, Tantur Ecumenical Institute, Jerusalem, 1 March 2008.

24 Kenneth Bailey used this phrase in a Bible reflection in Nazareth, at the sixth Sabeel International Conference, 'Forgotten Faithful', November 2006. It is this kind of scholarship and insight that permeates his book, *Jesus Through Middle Eastern Eyes* (London: SPCK, 2008).

25 Elias Chacour with Mary E. Jensen, *We Belong to the Land* (Notre Dame, IN: University of Notre Dame Press, 2001), p. 80.

26 Ilan Pappé, *The Ethnic Cleansing of Palestine* (Oxford: Oneworld, 2006); see also Nur Masalha, *The Bible and Zionism* (London: Zed Books, 2007).

27 These figures are diminishing all the time because of emigration.

28 Information taken from Rania Al Qass Collings, Rifat Odeh Kassis and Mitri Raheb (eds), *Palestinian Christians: Facts, Figures and Trends 2008* (Bethlehem: Diyar, 2008), Table 3, p. 10.

29 See Naim Ateek, 'The Future of Palestinian Christianity', in Naim Ateek, Cedar Duaybis and Maurine Tobin (eds), *The Forgotten Faithful: A Window into the Life and Witness of Christians in the Holy Land* (Jerusalem: Sabeel Ecumenical Liberation Theology Center, 2007), pp. 136–50, especially 139–40.

30 Michel Sabbah, speech in Jerusalem, November 2006, sixth Sabeel International Conference, 'Forgotten Faithful'. The written text, as published in *The Forgotten Faithful* (see above), is not as dramatic as his poignant speech on the occasion.

31 Archbishop Desmond Tutu, 'Palestine and Apartheid', Friends of Sabeel Conference, Boston, 27 October 2007.

32 This has already been called for by Patriarch Michel Sabbah in many of his speeches and writings, especially his farewell Pastoral Letter (1 March 2008).

1 John the Baptist – prophet of the Advent journey

1 Mahatma Gandhi, cited in Thomas Merton, *Conjectures of a Guilty Bystander* (London: Burns & Oates, 1995; Abbey of Gethsemani, 1965), p. 84.

2 There are other sources – for example, the Jewish historian, Josephus.

3 Christopher Hollis and Ronald Brownrigg, *Holy Places: Jewish, Christian and Muslim Monuments in the Holy Land* (London: Weidenfeld & Nicolson, 1969), pp. 132–3.

4 David Catchpole, personal conversation, and also in David Catchpole, *Jesus People: the Historical Jesus and the Beginnings of Community* (London: Darton, Longman & Todd, 2006), p. 20.

5 Catchpole, *Jesus People*, p. 23.

6 Luise Schottroff is opposed to the view of Theissen that the 'itinerant radicalism' of the Jesus movement was due to the voluntary renunciation of possessions; rather sheer poverty was the cause. Luise Schottroff, *Lydia's Impatient Sisters: A Feminist Social History of Early Christianity* (London: SCM Press, 1995), translated by Barbara and Martin Rumscheidt, pp. 7– 9.

7 Schottroff, *Lydia's Impatient Sisters*, pp. 92–3.

8 The parallels with India, especially with the desert state of Rajasthan, north-west India, are drawn from 22 years' experience as part of an NGO, Wells for India, that I helped to found in 1987. See <http://www.wellsforindia.org>.

9 See Joachim Jeremias, *Jerusalem in the Time of Jesus* (London: SCM Press, 1969), p. 308.

10 Michael Prior, *Jesus the Liberator: Nazareth Liberation Theology* (Sheffield: Sheffield Academic Press, 1995), pp. 173–5.

11 UN World Food Programme website: <http://www.wfp.org>.

12 Michael Evenari, Leslie Shanan and Naphtali Tadmor, *The Negev: The Challenge of a Desert* (Cambridge, MA: Harvard University Press, 1971/1982), p. 9.

13 Evenari et al., *The Negev*, pp. 9 10.

14 The statistics are from the UNEP Report, 'Global Environmental Outlook', prepared for the Summit on Sustainable Development, Johannesburg, 2002.

15 Hwaa Irfan, 'The Environmental Impact on the Occupied Palestinian Territories', at <http://www.islamonline.net>. Part of this section paraphrases much of the valuable information of this article, which is a summary of (mainly) the research at the Arab Research Institute, Jerusalem (or ARIJ), of Jad Isaac and Belgian researchers.

16 Mcm = thousands of cubic metres.

17 These figures are from B'Tselem, a Jerusalem-based human-rights organization, at the end of 2007.

18 Cited by Marq De Villiers, *Water Wars: Is the World's Water Running Out?* (London: Weidenfeld & Nicolson, 1999), p. 232.

19 All these figures have been cited recently by a video of the Arabic-language news network Al Jazeera on 27 October 2009, based on a report by Amnesty International. See <http://www.youtube.com/watch?v=OqUNyEcUGnQ>. Amnesty's allegations were denied by the Israeli government, but repeated by B'Tselem.

20 De Villiers, *Water Wars*, p. 234.

21 GDP = gross domestic product.

22 Matthew 3.16–17; Mark 1.9–11; Luke 3.22; John 1.29–34 – but John witnesses to Jesus and does not baptize.

23 The River Jordan has been the subject of a recent BBC radio documentary, *A River Runs through It*, by Edward Stourton, in September 2009. See the BBC Radio 4 website, where it is still available, together with a slide show.

24 See John 3.23: 'John also was baptizing at Aenon near Salim, because water was plentiful there, and people were coming and being baptized'.

25 See Hollis and Brownrigg, *Holy Places*, p. 128.

26 See the Epilogue to this book, pp. 110–20.

27 See Bargil Pixner, *With Jesus through Galilee According to the Fifth Gospel* (Israel: Corazin Publishing, 1992), pp. 20–1.

28 Kirsteen Kim, *Mission in the Spirit: The Holy Spirit in Indian Christian Theologies* (Delhi: ISPCK, 2003), pp. 97–9. She cites Sister Vandana, *Waters of Fire* (Bangalore: ATC; New York: Amity House, 1981).

29 Vandana: *Waters of Fire*, pp. 97–8.

30 Luke 3.10–14.

31 See http://www.christian-ecology.org.uk/loaf.htm.

32 See <http://www.tikkun.org>.

33 Christian Aid's work and outreach is similar.

34 See Thomas Berry, *Dream of the Earth* (San Francisco: Sierra Club, 1986); *The Great Work: Our Way into the Future* (New York: Bell Tower, 1999).

35 This is argued eloquently by Terrence J. Rynne, *Gandhi and Jesus: The Saving Power of Non-violence* (Maryknoll, NY: Orbis, 2008).

36 This is the cotton under-garment worn by traditional Indian peasants.

37 Even though the number has now diminished, over 60 per cent of Indians still live in villages.

38 See Mary Grey, *Sacred Longings: Ecofeminist Theology and Globalization* (London: SCM Press, 2003).

39 Here it has to be admitted that his stance on Untouchability, though sincere and well thought out, was opposed by the Dalits themselves. Gandhi refused to envisage a separate vote for Untouchables, because this would weaken the Hindu vote in relation to the Muslim: when he embarked on a fast-unto-death, the Dalit leader and hero, and co-writer of the constitution, himself a Dalit, Dr Ambedkar, had no option but to give in, such was Gandhi's stature.

2 The Annunciation

1 Mary Grey, 'Annunciation/Lady Day'. This has been set to music by June Boyce-Tillman, 'Hail full of Grace: A Hymn for Annunciation', in *A Rainbow to Heaven: Hymns, Songs and Chants* (London: Stainer & Bell, 2006), pp. 142–3. The wild goose is a symbol of the Spirit in both

Celtic and Hindu spiritualities. The poem depicts Mary as embodying Sophia (Wisdom/Spirit) and moving from the Annunciation experience to prophetic action. The voice alternates between Mary and God. (I retain copyright for the words.)

2 'The Greeks claim that the Annunciation took place not only at the site of the Latin Basilica but at Mary's Well, over which they have built their own church.' See Christopher Hollis and Ronald Brownrigg, *Holy Places* (London: Weidenfeld & Nicolson, 1969), p. 107. The source of this legend appears to be the apocryphal *Infancy Gospel of James*, or *Protoevangelion of James*.

3 John 1.46. These are the words of Nathanael.

4 Mark 6.4: 'And Jesus said to them, "A prophet is not without honour, except in his home town and among his relatives and in his own household." And he could do no mighty work there . . . And he marvelled because of their unbelief.'

5 Joshua 19.10–16.

6 Josephus, 37–100 AD.

7 Sources include <http://en.wikipedia.org/wiki/Nazareth> and personal notes from the seventh Sabeel International Conference, 'A Time to Remember, A Time for Truth: Al-Nakba', November 2008.

8 The archaeologist and priest, Fr Bellarmino Bagatti, uncovered pottery dating from the Middle Bronze Age (*c.*2200–1500 BC), and ceramics, silos and grinding mills from the Iron Age (*c.*1500–586 BC). Thus, there is no doubt that a substantial settlement existed in the Nazareth basin during those eras. However, lack of archaeological evidence from Assyrian, Babylonian, Persian, Hellenistic or Early Roman times, at least in the major excavations between 1955 and 1990, shows that the settlement apparently came to an abrupt end about 720 BC, when many towns in the area were destroyed by the Assyrians. Source: Wikipedia, 'Nazareth'. Fr Bagatti has been the principal archaeologist at Nazareth. His book, *Excavations in Nazareth* (Jerusalem: Franciscan Printing Press, 1969), is still the standard reference for the archaeology of the settlement, and is based on excavations at the Franciscan Venerated Area.

9 St Jerome, 342–420 AD.

10 St Jerome, *Commentary on Isaiah*, PL 22,574, cited in Bargil Pixner, *With Jesus through Galilee According to the Fifth Gospel* (Israel: Corazin Publishing, 1992), p. 14.

11 Pixner, *With Jesus*, p. 16.

12 According to the Israel Central Bureau of Statistics, Nazareth had a population of approximately 65,000 in 2005. The vast majority of its residents

are Arab citizens of Israel, 31.3 per cent of whom are Christians. Nazareth forms a metropolitan area with the Arab local councils of Yafa an-Naseriyye to the south, Reineh, Mashhad and Kafr Kanna to the north, Iksal and the adjacent city of Nazareth Illit to the east, which has a population of 40,000 Jews, and Ilut to the west. Together, the Nazareth metropolis area has a population of approximately 185,000, of whom over 125,000 are Israeli Arabs.

13 These were the words of Dr Ghattas, a consultant on strategic planning, at the seventh Sabeel International Conference, 'A Time to Remember, A Time for Truth: Al-Nakba', in November 2008.

14 Jeff Halper, *An Israeli in Palestine: Resisting Dispossession, Redeeming Israel* (London: Pluto Press, 2008).

15 John Dear, *Mary of Nazareth, Prophet of Peace* (Notre Dame, IN: Ave Maria Press, 2003).

16 See Luise Schottroff, *Lydia's Impatient Sisters: A Feminist Social History of Early Christianity* (London: SCM Press, 1995), translated by Barbara and Martin Rumscheidt.

17 Yvone Gebara and Maria Clara Bingemer, *Mary Mother of God and Mother of the Poor* (Maryknoll, NY: Orbis, 1989), translated by Philip Berryman. A similar focus is presented by the Sri Lankan theologian, Tissa Balasuriya, *Mary and Human Liberation* (London: Mowbray, 1997), ed. Helen Stanton. As we have discussed in Chapter 1, Elizabeth may also have had an obscured role in the composition of the Magnificat.

18 Rosemary Radford Ruether, *Mary: The Feminine Face of the Church* (London: SCM Press, 1979).

19 Grey, 'Annunciation/Lady Day' – see note 1.

20 Elizabeth Johnson, *Truly Our Sister: A Theology of Mary in the Communion of Saints* (New York: Continuum, 2004).

21 Johnson, *Truly Our Sister*, p. 256.

22 Pixner, *With Jesus*, pp. 51–2.

23 I leave to one side the idea of some recent theologians, such as Jane Schaberg, that Mary was raped, and Matthew's narrative of the agreement with Joseph an attempt to conceal it. See Jane Schaberg, *The Illegitimacy of Jesus: A Feminist Theological Interpretation of the Infancy Narratives* (New York: Crossroad, 1995). There is no evidence from tradition to support this theory. If it is an argument from silence, it is strange that scriptural writers have not been ashamed to cite rape and violence against other women where this has occurred (cf. Judges 19), and omit to mention this in a context of Mary's life.

24 Gerard Manley Hopkins, 'The Blessed Virgin Compared to the Air we Breathe', in *Poems and Prose of Gerard Manley Hopkins* (London: Penguin, 1953), p. 56.

25 The source used by the Medaille Community is Elzbieta M. Gozdziak and Elizabeth A. Collett, 'Research on Human Trafficking in North America: A Review of Literature', *International Migration*, vol. 43 (1/2), 2005. For the 2004 Trafficking in Persons report itself, see <http://www.state.gov/g/tip/rls/tiprpt/2004/index.htm>.

26 The Medaille Community is a group of religious sisters of the Community of St Joseph Medaille of Annecy in France. Begun in 1997, it moved from working with prostitutes in Southampton to setting up a safe house for trafficked women, in conjunction with the UK Home Office. The Medaille Trust was set up in 2006. It now has considerable support from other religious congregations, and its leader, Sister Ann Teresa, has led a seminar in Rome for the Pontifical Institute of Religious Congregations. See statistics in their annual Newsletters for 2007–2009; <http://www.medaille.co.uk/newsletter>.

27 Recent suggestions in the British press that the actual figures of trafficked women have been exaggerated met with a storm of protest from academics and women's organizations. It was, however, acknowledged that discrepancies arose because of the difficulty of acquiring accurate figures, as this is a fraught area and one of great humiliation and suffering for women.

28 The source for these factors is my personal contact with the Medaille Community, Southampton, as part of their Vision Group. See also <http://en.wikipedia.org/wiki/The_Medaille_Trust>.

29 John Taylor, *The Go Between God* (London: Collins, 1972).

30 Isabel Carter Heyward, *The Redemption of God: A Theology of Mutual Relation* (Washington, DC: University Press of America, 1982).

31 Philip Newell, *Listening for the Heartbeat of God: A Celtic Spirituality* (London: SPCK, 1997).

32 *Hodogetria* means 'She who shows the way'.

33 Rowan Williams, *Ponder These Things: Praying with Icons of the Virgin* (Norwich: Canterbury Press, 2002), p. 11.

34 Thomas Merton, *Conjectures of a Guilty Bystander* (London: Burns & Oates, 1995; Abbey of Gethsemani, 1965), p. 132.

35 Simone Weil, *Waiting on God* (London: Fontana, 1949), translated by Emma Crauford.

36 Sallie McFague, *Life Abundant: Rethinking Theology and Economy for a Planet in Peril* (Minneapolis, MN: Augsburg Fortress, 2001).

37 Rowan Williams, *Dostoevsky: Language, Faith and Fiction* (London: Continuum, 2008), p. 44; emphasis in original.

38 Mark Patrick Hederman, *Walkabout: Life as Holy Spirit* (Dublin: Columba Press, 2005), pp. 259–63.

39 Iris Murdoch, *Jackson's Dilemma* (London: Chatto & Windus, 1995).

40 Hederman, *Walkabout*, p. 257, quoting from 'That Nature is a Heraclitean Fire and of the Comfort of the Resurrection', in *Poems and Prose of Gerard Manley Hopkins*, p. 66.

41 Hederman, *Walkabout*, p. 258.

42 Dear, *Mary*, p. 27.

43 Grey, 'Annunciation/Lady Day' – see note 1.

44 Luke 1.39–56.

45 Luke 4.18–19. Jesus – or Luke – has edited the text, and inserted a line from Isaiah 58.6.

46 James Massey, *The Gospel According to Luke*, Dalit Bible Commentary, New Testament vol. 3 (New Delhi: Centre for Dalit Studies, 2007), pp. 69–75.

3 The Nativity

1 From 'Broken Town', by Martin John Nicholls. Full text in Appendix 1.

2 As with the disputes around Nazareth, there are still questions of accuracy around the Bethlehem stories. But since both Matthew and Luke see Bethlehem as the birthplace of Jesus, this is sufficient warrant for our discussion. For this chapter, Luke's story is the focus; for the Epilogue, it will be Matthew's. John's Gospel is also drawn on here.

3 Michael Finkel, 'Bethlehem 2007 A.D.', *National Geographic*, December 2007, pp. 1–10. It is cited here because of its graphic character and because it highlights the contentious nature of how the situation is reported. For a detailed account on the economic devastation brought by the Wall, see the PowerPoint presentation of the organization Open Bethlehem at <http://www.openbethlehem.org>.

4 Hamas is the Islamic Militant party in the West Bank and Gaza.

5 For a developed critique of Finkel's article, see Omar Tesdell (a Palestinian American and former volunteer at the International Center in Bethlehem, at <http://www.annadwa.org/en/index.php?option=com_content&task=view&id=44&Itemid=112>).

6 The Anastas family has now set up a souvenir and craft shop to create some income.

7 Finkel, 'Bethlehem 2007 A.D.'.

8 The Israeli lawyer and military judge in charge of the settlement legal issues, Major Adrian Agassi, argues that Israel has a biblical claim to the

territories. 'The land was given to us by the Bible and not by some United Nations.' Meron Rapoport, 'Land Belongs to the Jews, Says Israeli Army Judge', in *The Guardian*, Tuesday 27 October 2009.

9 The source for information on the Bedouins is <http://www.Palestine-family.net>, 'The Palestinian Bedouins', by Arthur Avendano. Some 60,000 Bedouin used to live in the Negev desert area, but after 1948 most fled to Jordan, leaving around 11,000. See Laura Storr, 'No Place to Call Home', in *Justice: Social Issues – a Catholic Perspective*, November/December 2009, pp. 50–1.

10 See UN Report at <http://www.un.org/unrwa/access/BedouinReport_May06.pdf>.

11 The Arab Education Institute (AEI) is funded by Pax Christi International.

12 Personal conversation with Toine van Teeffelen in Bethlehem.

13 This incident was referred to in the Introduction.

14 Luke's word is *polis*, city-state in the Greek classical world – but not quite the same meaning in occupied Palestine today.

15 I do not give much credence to the once-popular belief that Luke had privileged access to Mary, Jesus' mother, and therefore received the Annunciation story first-hand from her. After historical criticism became widespread, this story – sadly in the view of many people – ceased to have much credibility. Scholars like Conzelmann think the infancy narratives are a later addition and distract from Luke's real theology, which begins – like Mark's – with the Baptism, the Temptations and Preaching in the Synagogue. This does not distract from seeking a deeper meaning for Christmas and is consistent with Luke's theology of peace and reconciliation throughout his Gospel.

16 Personal communication with Toine van Teeffelen; emphasis added.

17 Similar services occur with local varieties throughout Europe; internationally there are many diverse cultural expressions.

18 See Christopher Hollis and Ronald Brownrigg, *Holy Places* (London: Weidenfeld & Nicolson, 1969), p. 99. James was one of the sons of Zebedee and one of the first apostles of Jesus. He became the leader of the Jerusalem community and was martyred in 44 AD.

19 Cited in Kenneth Bailey, *Jesus Through Middle Eastern Eyes* (London: SPCK, 2008), p. 34. These insights are on pp. 27–37. Reproduced by permission of SPCK and InterVarsity Press.

20 Personal communication with Toine van Teeffelen.

21 From the Arab Educational Institute's 'Bethlehem Community Book' page at <http://aeicenter.tripod.com/arabeducationalinstitute/id13.html>.

22 Again this is the insight of Bailey, *Jesus Through Middle Eastern Eyes*, p. 32.

23 Joachim Jeremias, *Jerusalem in the Time of Jesus* (London: SCM, 1969), p. 305.

24 W. H. Auden, 'At the Manger', from *For the Time Being – A Christmas Oratorio*, in *Collected Poems* (London: Faber & Faber, 1976). Reproduced by permission of Faber and Faber Ltd. 'For the Time Being', copyright 1944 and renewed 1972 by W. H. Auden, from COLLECTED POEMS OF W. H. AUDEN by W. H. Auden. Used by permission of Random House, Inc.

25 Auden, 'At the Manger'.

26 Bailey, *Jesus Through Middle Eastern Eyes*.

27 Matthew 6.10 – a more extended version than Luke's own.

28 Luke 2.1.

29 Virgil, Eclogue IV, in Virgil: *The Pastoral Poems* (Harmondsworth: Penguin, 1949), translated by E. V. Rieu, p. 57.

30 We shall see how Isaiah will continue to inspire all four evangelists.

31 See Hollis and Brownrigg, *Holy Places*, p. 99.

32 See UNRWA Report, 2006.

33 Delia Khano, 'A Shepherd from Bethlehem', from *This Week in Palestine*, at <http://www.palestine-family.net>.

34 The incident described took place when I was in Jerusalem, November 2008.

35 See Elisabeth Schüssler Fiorenza, *Miriam's Child, Sophia's Prophet* (New York: Continuum, 1994).

36 See Chapter 1.

37 Personal communication from Toine van Teeffelen:

Dutch composer Merlijn Twaalfhoven is active in writing music for orchestras, choirs and chamber music groups all over the world, but is most known by the remarkable projects he creates in unusual locations. He is now creating a collaboration of Palestinian musicians in Jordan, the West Bank and Holland. His intention is to highlight the cultural richness of Palestine and to stimulate more artistic contact between Europe and the Middle East.

38 Migration is on the increase for Muslims as well as Christians.

39 Peter Cole, 'Advent Litany', in *Network*, no. 98, March 2009, p. 18. Reproduced by permission.

40 This is based on an interview with Zoughbi Zoughbi in November 2008, at his office in Bethlehem.

41 The following ideas are from Zoughbi Zoughbi, '"Community Justice": – The Middle East', December 2006, at <http://alaslah.org/art>.

42 This, Zoughbi says, should be accompanied by a change in behaviour and a stop to the mutual dehumanization process.

43 Since 1995, Wi'am has been able to address 1,700 cases with 85 per cent success.

44 Zoughbi mentions that if they are unable to tackle any problem through mediation, they refer it to arbitration.

45 Zoughbi, '"Community Justice"'.

46 F. W. de Klerk, the former State President of South Africa, is still seen as an enabling figure in the struggle to end Apartheid.

47 *Sumud* is a key concept and will be developed later.

48 Zoughbi Zoughbi, 'Alternative Approaches to Retributive Justice: The Challenge to Reconciliation', December 2003, at <http://alaslah.org/pdf/Alternative.pdf>, quoting from 'Reconciliation: A Return to the God of Peace', by J. Cabazares, a Filipino poet. Reproduced by permission.

4 Gospel peacemaking and a lifestyle of non-violence – 'a little child shall lead them'

1 Isaiah 11.6.

2 'Nonviolence: The Only Rational Choice', at <http://www.mendonline.org/articles.html>, the website of MEND (Middle East Non-Violence and Democracy); emphasis added.

3 Luke 10.5–6, in *The New Testament*, translated by Nicholas King SJ (Stowmarket: Kevin Mayhew, 2004). 'When you enter a house, greet it; and if the house is worthy, let your peace come upon it. Otherwise, let your peace return to you' Matthew 10.12–15, from the same translation.

4 Rabbi Michael Lerner, editor of *Tikkun*, from general e-mail of 23 September, 2008; emphasis added.

5 Luke 19.41–42.

6 This is a very ancient shrine. Relics of the prophet Muhammad are contained in a gilded reliquary. 'The visitor can touch the Rock where Muslim tradition identifies the footprint of the prophet.' Kay Prag, *Israel and the Palestine Territories: The Blue Guide* (London: A. & C. Black, 2002), p. 124.

7 See Mary Grey, 'The Dis-enchantment and Re-enchantment of Childhood in an Age of Globalization', in *International Journal of Children's Spirituality*, vol. 11, no. 1, April 2006, pp. 11–21.

8 Of India's 310 million children, 87 million do not go to school and 13 million are homeless.

9 China Keitetsi, 'Child Soldier', a story told in *The Big Issue*, 7–13 June 2004, pp. 8–9, based on the book of the same title (Souvenir Press, 2004).

10 K. Montgomery, 'Digital Kids: The New Online Children's Consumer Culture', in Cecilia von Feilitzen and Ulla Carlsson (eds), *Children, Young People and Media Globalisation* (Göteborg: Nordicom and UNESCO, 2002), pp. 189–208. The website referred to in this article is <http://www.mama-media.com>.

11 James U. McNeal, *The Kids Market: Myths and Realities* (Ithaca, NJ: Paramount Market, 1999), pp. 92–3.

12 Montgomery, 'Digital Kids', p. 199.

13 Of course it has to be admitted, as John Hull has described, that if the market co-opts the language of developmental psychology, and hijacks spirituality, some developmental psychologists have also co-opted the language of the market. (John Hull, 'Human Development and Capitalist Society', in James W. Fowler, Karl Ernst Nipkow and Friedrich Schweitzer (eds), *Stages of Faith and Religious Development: Implications for Church, Education and Society* (London: SCM Press, 1992), pp. 209–23).

14 F. Nyamnjoh, attributes this to Soyinka in 'Children, Media and Globalisation', in von Feilitzen and Carlsson, *Children, Young People and Media Globalisation*, pp. 43–52.

15 This is not to deny some positive effects of better media communication; for example, mobile phones in poor desert communities.

16 Nyamnjoh, 'Children, Media and Globalisation', p. 46.

17 Susan Linn, 'Sages for Sale' *Tikkun*, vol. 20, no. 4, July/August 2005, p. 62.

18 Suggestions for alternative gifts are presented in Appendix 2.

19 See <http://www.childrensparliament.org.uk/>.

20 See <http://www.gaiagroup.org/Research/facilitation/eco-city/>.

21 See <http://oiyp.oxfam.org/oiyp/index.html>.

22 Hospitality as part of Christmas celebrations will be explored in the next chapter.

23 Each of these features appears frequently in favourite stories of children. They are of course qualities of childhood, *where children are allowed to be children*.

24 Frances Hodgson Burnett, *The Secret Garden* (London: Wordsworth, 1993).

25 Rosemary Haughton, *Tales from Eternity* (London: Allen & Unwin, 1973), p. 16.

26 66–70 AD – thus before the Fall of Jerusalem and the Diaspora.

27 This theology of Mark is inspired particularly by Ched Myers, *Binding the Strong Man: A Political Reading of Mark's Story of Jesus* (Maryknoll, NY: Orbis, 2008), 20th anniversary edn.

28 See Chapters 1 and 2.

29 Myers, *Binding the Strong Man*, pp. 266–71.

30 Myers, *Binding the Strong Man*, p. 271.

31 Gandhi was born on 2 October 1869. This day is celebrated as the International Day of Non-Violence.

32 See Matthew 12.46–50; Mark 3.31–35; Luke 8.19–21.

33 For a study of the family through the ages, and a Christian revisioning of the nuclear family model, see Rosemary Radford Ruether, *Christianity and the Making of the Modern Family* (London: SCM Press, 2001).

34 See Chapter 1, note 39, p. 128, on Untouchability.

35 The best source for this is Terrence J. Rynne, *Gandhi and Jesus: The Saving Power of Nonviolence* (Maryknoll, NY: Orbis, 2008).

36 John 14.26; 17.17–19.

37 This happened when Gandhi led his followers in the Non-Cooperation Movement that protested against the British-imposed salt tax with the 400-km (249-mile) Dandi Salt March in 1930.

38 Yet it should not be forgotten that women played a key role in Gandhi's activism and *satyagraha* protests.

39 Matthew 26.51; Mark 14.47; John 18.10–11.

40 Matthew 10.9–14; Luke 9.3–5.

41 And not homosexuality as such.

42 Interestingly, the Markan Jesus – but not Matthew – tells the woman to go in peace. Matthew says rather 'take heart' (Matt. 9.18–26; Mark 5.21–43).

43 See Luise Schottroff, *Lydia's Impatient Sisters: A Feminist Social History of Early Christianity* (London: SCM Press, 1995), translated by Barbara and Martin Rumscheidt, pp. 112–15.

44 Tawfiq Canaan, in his 1922 paper, *Haunted Springs and Water Demons in Palestine* (see <http://commons.wikimedia.org/wiki/Haunted_Springs_and_Water_Demons_in_Palestine,_1922>), researched the perception of the origin of demons: he took the traditional view that they were once deities within the polytheistic system, or what Canaan refers to as 'primitive religions'. With the advent of monotheism, the status of these gods diminished, subsisting nevertheless in the community unconscious as demons. Demons (or jinns) especially haunted lonely places, caves, cracks in the earth where the sun could not reach.

45 John Howard Yoder, cited in Rynne, *Gandhi and Jesus*, p. 102.

46 Mahatma Gandhi, cited in Rynne, *Gandhi and Jesus*, p. 66.

47 The genealogy of influence of this text goes from Tolstoy to Gandhi, then to Martin Luther King and to Archbishop Desmond Tutu. Gandhi inspired the current American president, Barack Obama.

48 Cited in *Reflections in the Galilee* (Jerusalem: Sabeel Ecumenical Liberation Theology Center, 2008), p. 7, quoting from Elias Chacour with Mary E. Jensen, *We Belong to the Land* (Notre Dame, IN: University of Notre Dame Press, 2001), pp. 143–4.

49 For a note on Sabeel, see the Introduction, n. 5, p. 124; also <http://www.sabeel.org/index.php>.

50 This term was introduced in Chapter 2.

51 See Josef Ben-Eliezer, *My Search* (Farmington, PA and Robertsbridge, East Sussex: Plough Publishing House, 2007). This is a free e-book, available at <http://www.ploughbooks.co.uk>. The Bruderhof is now renamed Church Communities International.

52 Pastor Mitri Raheb is the director of the International Center of Bethlehem (ICB) briefly discussed in Chapter 2.

53 Mitri Raheb, *I am a Palestinian Christian* (Minneapolis, MN: Augsburg Fortress, 1995), p. 111.

54 Jean Zaru, *Occupied with Nonviolence: A Palestinian Woman Speaks* (Minneapolis, MN: Fortress Press, 2008), p. 72.

55 Zaru, *Occupied with Nonviolence*, pp. 72–3.

56 See Mary Grey, 'Deep Breath: Taking a Deep Breath: Spiritual Resources for a Pedagogy of Hope', in Toine van Teeffelen (ed.), *Challenging the Wall: Toward a Pedagogy of Hope* (Bethlehem: Arab Educational Institute – Open Windows, 2008), pp. 9–10.

57 Mitri Raheb, 'Culture as the Art to Breathe', <http://www.brightstars-bethlehem.org/index2.php?option=com_content&do_pdf=1&id=19>; also, 'Culture: Culture as the Art of Breathing', in van Teeffelen, *Challenging the Wall*, p. 18.

58 Toine van Teeffelen and Fuad Giacaman, 'Sumud: Resistance in Daily Life', in van Teeffelen, *Challenging the Wall*, p. 30.

59 See also Matthew 10.22: 'But the one who endures to the end will be saved.'

60 Thomas Traherne, 'The News', in Margery Willey, *The Metaphysical Poets* (London: Edward Arnold, 1971), p. 126.

61 Anne Primavesi, *Gaia's Gift: Earth, Ourselves and God after Copernicus* (London: Routledge, 2003).

62 Miroslav Volf, *Free of Charge: Giving and Forgiving in a Culture Stripped of Grace* (Grand Rapids, MI: Zondervan, 2005), p. 72.

63 See suggestions made in Appendix 2.

64 This story was told to me personally in the Peace House at Bethlehem.
It is also told in Riet Bons-Storm (ed.), *Vertel onze Verhalen Verder:
Ontmoetingen met Joodse en Palestijnse Vrouwen* (Gorinchem: Narratio,
2008).

5 Christmas Day – celebrating the feast

1 Isak Dinesen (Karen Blixen), 'Babette's Feast', in *Anecdotes of Destiny*
(London: Penguin, 1986), p. 61.

2 Harvey Cox, *The Feast of Fools* (New York: Harper & Row, 1969), pp. 22–3;
emphasis added.

3 *The Little Flowers of St Francis* (New York: Image Book/Doubleday, 1958),
ed. and intr. Raphael Brown, pp. 72–3.

4 See Robert Karris, *Eating your Way through Luke's Gospel* (Collegeville,
MN: Liturgical Press, 2006); Eugene LaVerdière, *Dining in the Kingdom
of God: The Origins of the Eucharist in the Gospel of Luke* (Chicago:
Liturgical Training Publications, 1994).

5 Chai is hot, sweet, milky tea.

6 Leviticus 19.33–34.

7 Jean Zaru, *Occupied with Nonviolence: A Palestinian Woman Speaks*
(Minneapolis, MN: Augsburg Fortress, 2008). The same notion was
explored in connection with Zoughbi Zoughbi and the work of Wi'am
in Bethlehem. See pp. 67–9.

8 Luke 24; John 21.

9 Karris, *Eating your Way through Luke's Gospel*, p. 12.

10 Matthew 14.13–21; Mark 6.32–34; Luke 9.11–17; John 6.1–14.

11 On the genealogy of influence of this sermon from Tolstoy onwards, see
Chapter 4, p. 137, note 47. It still sends ripples to the future.

12 Elias Chacour with Mary E. Jensen, *We Belong to the Land: The Story of
a Palestinian Israeli who Lives for Peace and Reconciliation* (Notre Dame,
IN: University of Notre Dame Press, 2001); Elias Chacour with David
Hazard, *Blood Brothers* (New York: Chosen Books, 1984).

13 Luke 9.11.

14 See, for example, Tissa Balasuriya, *The Eucharist and Human Liberation*
(London: SCM Press, 1979); Monika Hellwig, *The Eucharist and the Hunger
of the World* (New York: Paulist Press, 1976); Rafael Avila, *Worship and
Politics* (Maryknoll, NY: Orbis, 1977), translated by Alan Neely; Thomas
Cullinan, *The Passion of Political Love* (London: Sheed & Ward, 1987).

15 These statistics are from the third UNEP Global Environmental Outlook
report prepared for the Summit on Sustainable Development, Johannesburg,
2002, *GEO-3: Global Environmental Outlook* (Nairobi: UNEP, 2002).

16 Kenneth Bailey, *Jesus Through Middle Eastern Eyes* (London: SPCK, 2008), pp. 309–20.

17 Kenneth Bailey points out (in *Jesus Through Middle Eastern Eyes*) that in three contemporary sources (the Targums, the Book of Enoch and the Messianic Rule of the Qumran community), that this story had lost its lustre in New Testament times. How important then that Jesus introduces this new interpretation!

18 Cited in Bailey, *Jesus Through Middle Eastern Eyes*, p. 318.

19 I omit discussion of other dimensions of meals as settings for teaching and forgiveness because the focus here is primarily on festivity.

20 Richard Becher, 'The Parable of a Christmas Banquet', in Geoffrey Duncan (compiler), *Shine on, Star of Bethlehem: A Worship Resource for Advent, Christmas and Epiphany* (Norwich: Canterbury Press, 2001), pp. 222–3.

21 Mitri Raheb, *I am a Palestinian Christian* (Minneapolis, MN: Augsburg Fortress, 1995), p. 106.

22 This material is from Ron Kronish, 'Interreligious Dialogue in the Service of Peace', in *Cross Currents*, vol. 58, no. 2, summer 2008, pp. 224–46.

23 Kronish, 'Interreligious Dialogue', pp. 234–5.

24 I do not discuss the Farewell Meal and Passover because here the focus is on Christmas, and Passover is far more connected with Jesus' death and Resurrection.

25 Charles Dickens, *A Christmas Carol* (London: Wordsworth, 1993).

26 I wrote this on returning home, November 2008.

27 The number of descendants of Palestinian refugees by country as of 2005 were as follows: Jordan 1,827,877 refugees, Gaza 986,034 refugees, West Bank 699,817 refugees, Syria 432,048 refugees, Lebanon 404,170 refugees, Saudi Arabia 240,000 refugees, Egypt 70,245 refugees.

28 Source is <http://en.wikipedia.org/wiki/Palestine_refugee>.

29 See Mary Grey, *To Rwanda and Back: Liberation Spirituality and Reconciliation* (London: Darton, Longman & Todd, 2007). This visit was referred to earlier in this chapter, p. 100.

30 See 'Saving Sanctuary' (May 2008), 'Safe Return' (June 2008), 'Deserving Dignity' (July 2008), reports from the Independent Asylum Commission's review of the UK asylum system, at <http://www.independentasylumcommission.org.uk/>.

31 Catholic Bishops' Conference of England and Wales, *Mission of the Church to Migrants in England and Wales* (London: Catholic Truth Society, 2008).

32 For some of these points I am indebted to Canon Nicholas Sagovsky, 'Asylum, Human Rights and Christian Theology', unpublished talk at Las Casas Institute, Blackfriars, Oxford, 2008.

33 Thomas Merton, 'Hagia Sophia', in *Emblems of a Season of Fury* (Norfolk, CT: J. Laughlin, 1963), cited in Mary Grey, Andrée Heaton and Danny Sullivan (eds), *The Candles are Still Burning* (London: Cassell, 1994), p. 171.

34 Translated by Fuad Giacaman, composed and written by Fr Mansour Labki of Lebanon. '*Leilat al-Milad*' may be found at <http://www.palestine-family.net>. Reproduced by permission.

Epilogue: Epiphany – the journey carries on

1 There are many sources for this story: this is based on 'The Legend of Baboushka', in *Fairy Tales and Legends of the World* (Manchester: World Distributors, 1967), compiled and retold by Mae Bradley, pp. 102–4.

2 The whole passage is redolent of Epiphany symbolism. For the idea of the newborn King, Matthew cites Jeremiah 23.5 and Zechariah 9.9.

3 See Susan K. Roll, *Towards the Origins of Christmas* (Kampen: Kok Pharos, 1995).

4 See Chapter 1, pp. 27–8. The Orthodox Church considers Jesus' baptism to be the first step towards the Crucifixion, and there are some parallels in the hymnography used on this day and the hymns chanted on Good Friday.

5 I am omitting here, because my focus is the outcome of this journey, the folk traditions around Epiphany, both positive, like making Three Kings' cake (popular in France), and other customs, slanted towards commercialization, like the groups of children singing outside houses to collect money, or the collection of gold inside Anglican cathedrals. Admittedly the latter is oriented towards charitable giving.

6 James Joyce, *A Portrait of the Artist as a Young Man* (London: Wordsworth, 1992).

7 James Joyce, *Dubliners* (London: Wordsworth, 1993).

8 Emmanuel Levinas, 'Ethics as First Philosophy', in Seán Hand (ed.), *The Levinas Reader* (Oxford: Blackwell, 1989), p. 83.

9 See Chapter 2.

10 What follows here is inspired by a correspondence between myself and Rabbi Dan Cohn-Sherbok, September 2009, a redacted version of which appeared in *The Tablet* under the heading 'A Time to Embrace', 19–26 December 2009, pp. 20–1.

11 Sura 19.16–35.

12 Personal communication from Toine van Teeffelen, education director of the Arab Educational Institute in Bethlehem.

13 Rabbi Dan Cohn-Sherbok – see note 10.

14 Rabbi Dan Cohn-Sherbok – see note 10.

15 Rabbi Dan Cohn-Sherbok – see note 10.

16 From ON THE PULSE OF THE MORNING by Maya Angelou, copyright © 1993 by Maya Angelou. Used by permission of Random House, Inc.

17 Rabbi Dan Cohn-Sherbok – see note 10.

18 Mark Braverman, 'Zionism and Post-Holocaust Christian Theology: A Jewish Perspective', in *Holy Land Studies*, 8.1, 2009, p. 32.

19 The title of the 6th Sabeel International Conference in Jerusalem and the West Bank in November 2006.

20 Lydia Baker (and colleagues), *Feeling the Heat: Child Survival in a Changing Climate* (London: Save the Children International, 2009), p. vi.

21 Peter Cornelius, 'Three Kings from Persian Lands Afar', in *The Oxford Book of Carols* (Oxford: Oxford University Press, 1964), p. 423, no. 193.

22 As cited by Rabbi Dan Cohn-Sherbok – see note 10.

23 This is the best way to avoid needless cutting down of millions of fir trees every year.

24 Reprinted with permission from Friends United Press, from 'The Work of Christmas' by Howard Thurman, in *The Mood of Christmas* (Richmond, IN: Friends United Press, 1985).

25 W. H. Auden, 'At the Manger', from *For the Time Being – A Christmas Oratorio*, in *Collected Poems* (London: Faber & Faber, 1976). Reproduced by permission of Faber and Faber Ltd. 'For the Time Being', copyright 1944 and renewed 1972 by W. H. Auden, from COLLECTED POEMS OF W. H. AUDEN by W. H. Auden. Used by permission of Random House, Inc.

Further reading

Scriptural resources

Bailey, Kenneth, *Jesus Through, Middle Eastern Eyes* (London: SPCK, 2008).

Catchpole, David, *Jesus People: the Historical Jesus and the Beginnings of Community* (London: Darton, Longman & Todd, 2006).

Fiorenza, Elisabeth Schüssler, *Miriam's Child, Sophia's Prophet* (New York: Continuum, 1994).

Hollis, Christopher and Ronald Brownrigg, *Holy Places: Jewish, Christian and Muslim Monuments in the Holy Land* (London: Weidenfeld & Nicolson, 1969).

Jeremias, Joachim, *Jerusalem in the Time of Jesus* (London: SCM Press, 1969), translated by F. H. and C. H. Cave.

Johnson, Elizabeth, *Truly Our Sister: a Theology of Mary in the Communion of Saints* (New York: Continuum, 2004).

Kim, Kirsteen, *Mission in the Spirit: The Holy Spirit in Indian Christian Theologies* (Delhi: ISPCK, 2003).

Kopp, Clemens, *The Holy Places of the Gospel* (New York: Herder & Herder, 1963).

Massey, James, *The Gospel According to Luke*, in Dalit Bible Commentary, vol. 3 (New Delhi: Centre for Bible Studies, 2007).

Myers, Ched, *Binding the Strong Man: A Political Reading of Mark's Story of Jesus* (Maryknoll, NY: Orbis, 2008), 20th anniversary edn.

Pixner, Bargil, *With Jesus through Galilee According to the Fifth Gospel* (Israel: Corazin, 1992).

Prior, Michael, *Jesus the Liberator: Nazareth Liberation Theology* (Sheffield: Sheffield Academic Press, 1995).

Roll, Susan, *Toward the Origins of Christmas* (Kampen: Kok Pharos, 1995).

Ruether, Rosemary Radford, *Mary: The Feminine Face of the Church* (London: SCM Press, 1979).

Schaberg, Jane, *The Illegitimacy of Jesus: A Feminist Theological Interpretation of the Infancy Narratives* (New York: Crossroad, 1995).

Schottroff, Luise, *Lydia's Impatient Sisters: A Feminist Social History of Early Christianity* (London: SCM Press, 1995), translated by Barbara and Martin Rumscheidt.

Vandana, Sister, *Waters of Fire* (Bangalore: ATC; New York: Amity House, 1981).

Wright, Tom, *Luke for Everyone* (London: SPCK, 2001).

Wright, Tom, *Mark for Everyone* (London: SPCK, 2001).

Wright, Tom, *Matthew for Everyone* (London: SPCK, 2002).

Peace in the Middle East

Ateek, Naim, *Justice and Only Justice* (Maryknoll, NY: Orbis, 1989).

Ateek, Naim, *A Palestinian Christian Cry for Reconciliation* (Maryknoll, NY: Orbis, 2008).

Ateek, Naim (ed.), *Challenging Christian Zionism: Theology, Politics and the Israel–Palestine Conflict* (London: Melisende, 2005).

Ateek, Naim, Cedar Duaybis and Maurine Tobin (eds), *The Forgotten Faithful: A Window into the Life and Witness of Christians in the Holy Land* (Jerusalem: Sabeel Ecumenical Liberation Theology Centre, 2007).

Avnery, Uri, 'Uri Avnery on How to Create Israeli-Palestinian Peace', *Tikkun*, January/February 2009, pp. 29–30.

Awad, Sami, unpublished lecture, 'Vanishing Palestine Conference', organized by the Amos Trust, All Hallows on the Wall Church, London, 22 September 2008.

Bergen, Kathy, 'Lamenting the Destruction: the Nakba Continues', in *Cornerstone*, 49, summer 2008, pp. 10–11.

Bons-Storm, Riet (ed.), *Vertel onze Verhalen Verder: Ontmoetingen met Jodie en Palestine Rouen* (Grinch: Narration, 2008).

Braverman, Mark, 'Zionism and Post Holocaust Christian Theology: A Jewish Perspective', in *Holy Land Studies*, 8.1, 2009, pp. 31–54.

Burge, Gary, *Whose Land? Whose Promise? What Christians Are Not Being Told About Israel and the Palestinians*, 2nd edn (Cleveland, OH: Pilgrims Press, 2003).

Chacour, Elias, with David Hazard, *Blood Brothers* (New York: Chosen Books, 1984).

Chacour, Elias, with Mary E. Jensen, *We Belong to the Land: The Story of a Palestinian Israeli who Lives for Peace and Reconciliation* (Notre Dame, IN: University of Notre Dame Press, 2001).

Dear, John, *Mary of Nazareth, Prophet of Peace* (Notre Dame, IN: Ave Maria Press, 2003).

Dear, John, *Put Down your Sword: Answering the Gospel Call to Creative Nonviolence* (Grand Rapids, MI: Eerdmans, 2008).

Finkel, Michael, 'Bethlehem 2007 A.D.' *National Geographic*, December 2007, pp. 1–10.

Further reading

Halper, Jeff, *An Israeli in Palestine: Resisting Dispossession, Redeeming Israel* (London: Pluto Press, 2008).

Herzl, Theodor, *Der Judenstaat: Versuch einer Modernen Lösung der Judenfrage* (Leipzig and Vienna: Breitenstein, 1896); English translation, *The Jewish State* (New York: Dover, 1988).

Hewitt, Garth, *Bethlehem Speaks: Voices from the Little Town Cry Out* (London: SPCK, 2008).

Irfan, Hwaa, 'The Environmental Impact on the Occupied Palestinian Territories', at <www.islamonline.net>.

Kronish, Ron, 'Interreligious Dialogue in the Service of Peace', in *Cross Currents*, vol. 58, no. 2, Summer 2008, pp. 224–46.

Lerner, Michael, *Healing Israel/Palestine: A Path to Peace and Reconciliation* (Berkeley, CA: Tikkun Books, 2003).

Marchadour, Alain and David Neuhaus, *The Land, the Bible and History: Toward the Land That I will Show You* (New York: Fordham University Press, 2007).

Masalha, Nur, *The Bible and Zionism* (London: Zed Books, 2007).

Pappé, Ilan, *The Ethnic Cleansing of Palestine* (Oxford: Oneworld, 2006).

Prag, Kay, *Israel and the Palestine Territories: The Blue Guide* (London: A. & C. Black, 2002).

Prior, Michael, CM, *A Living Stone: Selected Essays and Addresses*, ed. Duncan Macpherson (London: Living Stones of the Holy Land Trust and Melisende, 2006).

Raheb, Mitri, *Bethlehem Besieged: Stories of Hope in Times of Trouble* (Minneapolis, MN: Augsburg Fortress, 2004).

Raheb, Mitri, *I am a Palestinian Christian* (Minneapolis, MN: Augsburg Fortress, 1995).

Rynne, Terrence J., *Gandhi and Jesus: The Saving Power of Non-violence* (Maryknoll, NY: Orbis, 2008).

Said, Edward, *Peace and its Discontents: Gaza-Jericho, 1993–1995* (London: Vintage, 1995).

Sizer, Stephen, *Christian Zionism: Road-Map to Armageddon?* (Leicester: InterVarsity Press, 2004).

Storr, Laura, 'No Place to Call Home', in *Justice: Social Issues – a Catholic Perspective* November/December 2009, pp. 50–1.

Teeffelen, Toine van (ed.), *Challenging the Wall: Toward a Pedagogy of Hope* (Bethlehem: Arab Educational Institute – Open Windows, 2008).

Tutu, Archbishop Desmond, 'Palestine and Apartheid', Friends of Sabeel Conference, Boston USA, 27 October, 2007.

Zaru, Jean, *Occupied with Nonviolence: A Palestinian Woman Speaks* (Minneapolis, MN: Augsburg Fortress, 2008).

Zoughbi, Zoughbi, 'Alternative Approaches to Retributive Justice: The Challenge to Reconciliation', December 2003, at <http://alaslah.org/pdf/ Alternative.pdf>, citing Filipino poet, J. Cabazares.

Other miscellaneous resources

Angelou, Maya, 'On the Pulse of the Morning', in *The Complete Collected Poems of Maya Angelou* (New York: Random House, 1993).

Auden, W. H., 'At the Manger', from *For the Time Being – A Christmas Oratorio*, in *Collected Poems* (London: Faber & Faber, 1976).

Baker, Lydia (and colleagues), *Feeling the Heat: Child Survival in a Changing Climate* (London: Save the Children International, 2009).

Berry, Thomas, *Dream of the Earth* (San Francisco, CA: The Sierra Club, 1986).

Boyce-Tillman, June, 'Hail Full of Grace: A Hymn for Annunciation', in *A Rainbow to Heaven: Hymns, Songs and Chants* (London: Stainer & Bell, 2006), pp. 142–3.

Bradley, Mae (compiler and reteller), *Fairy Tales and Legends of the World* (Manchester: World Distributors, 1967).

Brown, Raphael (ed.), *The Little Flowers of St Francis* (New York: Image Book/ Doubleday, 1958).

Burnett, Frances Hodgson, *The Secret Garden* (London: Wordsworth, 1993).

Cardenal, Rodolfo, SJ, 'The Crucified People', in Mary Grey (ed.), *Reclaiming Vision: Education, Liberation and Justice* (Southampton: Centre for Contemporary Theology, 1994), pp. 12–18.

Catholic Bishops' Conference of England and Wales, *Mission of the Church to Migrants in England and Wales* (London: Catholic Truth Society, 2008).

Cole, Peter, 'Advent Litany', in *Network*, no. 98, March 2009, p. 18.

Cornelius, Peter, 'Three Kings from Persian Lands afar', in *The Oxford Book of Carols* (Oxford: Oxford University Press, 1964), p. 423, no. 193.

Cox, Harvey, *The Feast of Fools* (New York: Harper & Row, 1969).

De Villiers, Marq, *Water Wars: Is the World's Water Running out?* (London: Weidenfeld & Nicolson, 1999).

Dinesen, Isak (Karen Blixen), 'Babette's Feast', in *Anecdotes of Destiny* (London: Penguin, 1986), pp. 23–68.

Duncan, Geoffrey (compiler), *Shine on, Star of Bethlehem: A Worship Resource for Advent, Christmas and Epiphany* (Norwich: Canterbury Press, 2001).

Further reading

Evenari, Michael, Leslie Shanan and Naphthali Tadmor, *The Negev: The Challenge of a Desert* (Cambridge, MA: Harvard University Press, 1971/1982).

Finlay, Fergus, *Mary Robinson: President with a Purpose* (Dublin: O'Brien Press, 1990).

Fowler, James W., Karl Ernst Nipkow and Friedrich Schweitzer (eds), *Stages of Faith and Religious Development: Implications for Church, Education and Society* (London: SCM Press, 1992).

Gozdziak, Elzbieta M. and Elizabeth A. Collett, 'Research on Human Trafficking in North America: A Review of Literature', *International Migration*, vol. 43 (1/2), 2005.

Grey, Mary, 'The Dis-enchantment and Re-enchantment of Childhood in an Age of Globalization', in *International Journal of Children's Spirituality*, vol. 11, no. 1, April 2006, pp. 11–21.

Grey, Mary, *To Rwanda and Back: Liberation Spirituality and Reconciliation* (London: Darton, Longman & Todd, 2007).

Grey, Mary, 'Deep Breath: Taking a Deep Breath: Spiritual Resources for a Pedagogy of Hope', in Toine van Teeffelen (ed.), *Challenging the Wall: Toward a Pedagogy of Hope* (Bethlehem: Arab Educational Institute – Open Windows, 2008), pp. 9–15.

Grey, Mary (ed.), *Reclaiming Vision: Education, Liberation and Justice* (Southampton: Centre for Contemporary Theology, 1994).

Grey, Mary, Andrée Heaton and Danny Sullivan (eds), *The Candles are Still Burning* (London: Cassell, 1994).

Gupta, Rahila, *Enslaved: The New British Slavery* (London: Portobello Books, 2007).

Hand, Seán (ed.), *The Levinas Reader* (Oxford: Blackwell, 1989).

Haughton, Rosemary, *Tales from Eternity* (London: Allen & Unwin, 1973).

Hederman, Mark Patrick, *Walkabout: Life as Holy Spirit* (Dublin: Columba Press, 2005).

Heyward, Isabel Carter, *The Redemption of God: A Theology of Mutual Relation* (Washington, DC: University Press of America, 1982).

Heyward, Isabel Carter, *Our Passion for Justice* (New York: Pilgrim Press, 1984).

Heyward, Carter and Anne Gilson, *Revolutionary Forgiveness: Feminist Reflections on Nicaragua* (Maryknoll, NY: Orbis, 1987).

Hopkins, Gerard Manley, *Poems and Prose of Gerard Manley Hopkins* (London: Penguin, 1953).

Horsley, Richard and James Tracy (eds), *Christmas Unwrapped: Consumerism, Christ and Culture* (Harrisburg, PA: Trinity Press International, 2001).

Further reading

Hull, John, 'Human Development and Capitalist Society', in Fowler et al., *Stages of Faith*, pp. 209–23.

Hutch, Richard A., *The Meaning of Lives: Biography, Autobiography and the Spiritual Quest* (London: Continuum, 1997).

Independent Asylum Commission, reports from the Commission's review of the UK asylum system, 'Saving Sanctuary' (May 2008), 'Safe Return' (June 2008), 'Deserving Dignity' (July 2008), at <http://www.independentasylumcommission.org.uk/>.

Joyce, James, *A Portrait of the Artist as a Young Man* (London: Wordsworth, 1992).

Keitetsi, C., 'Child Soldier', a story told in *The Big Issue*, 7–13 June, 2004, pp. 8–9, based on the book of the same title (Souvenir Press, 2004).

Linn, Susan, 'Sages for Sale', *Tikkun*, vol. 20, no. 4, July/August 2005, p. 62.

McNeal, James U., *The Kids Market: Myths and Realities* (Ithaca, NJ: Paramount Market, 1999).

Merton, Thomas, 'Hagia Sophia', in *Emblems of a Season of Fury* (Norfolk, CT: J. Laughlin, 1963), cited in Grey et al., *The Candles are Still Burning*, p. 171.

Merton, Thomas, *Conjectures of a Guilty Bystander* (London: Burns & Oates, 1995; Abbey of Gethsemani, 1965).

Newell, Philip, *Listening for the Heartbeat of God: A Celtic Spirituality* (London: SPCK, 1997).

Murdoch, Iris, *Jackson's Dilemma* (London: Chatto & Windus, 1995).

Nyamnjoh, F., 'Children, Media and Globalisation', in von Feilitzen and Carlsson, *Children, Young People and Media Globalisation*, pp. 43–52.

Primavesi, Anne, *Gaia's Gift: Earth, Ourselves and God after Copernicus* (London: Routledge, 2003).

Ruether, Rosemary Radford, *Christianity and the Making of the Modern Family* (London: SCM Press, 2001).

Sagovsky, Nicholas, 'Asylum, Human Rights and Christian Theology', unpublished talk at Las Casas Institute, Blackfriars, Oxford, 2008.

Slee, Nicola and Rosie Miles, *Doing December Differently: An Alternative Christmas Handbook* (Glasgow: Wild Goose, 2006).

Volf, Miroslav, *Free of Charge: Giving and Forgiving in a Culture Stripped of Grace* (Grand Rapids, MI: Zondervan, 2005).

Von Feilitzen, Cecilia and Ulla Carlsson (eds), *Children, Young People and Media Globalisation* (Göteborg: Nordicom and UNESCO, 2002).

Weil, Simone, *Waiting on God* (London: Fontana, 1949), translated by Emma Crauford.

Williams, Rowan, *Ponder These Things: Praying with Icons of the Virgin* (Norwich: Canterbury Press, 2002).

Williams, Rowan, *Dostoevsky: Language, Faith and Fiction* (London: Continuum, 2008).

Websites

http://alaslah.org/art
http://en.wikipedia.org/wiki/Epiphany
http://en.wikipedia.org/wiki/The_Medaille_Trust
http://en.wikipedia.org/wiki/Nazareth
http://en.wikipedia.org/wiki/Palestine_refugee
http://jerusalemprayerteam.org/pdf/022505.pdf 'William Blackstone, Defender of the Jews'
http://www.aeicenter.org – Arab Educational Center, Bethlehem
http://www.annadwa.org – International Center of Bethlehem
http://www.annadwa.org/en/index.php?option=com_content&task=view&id=44&Itemid=112 – Response to Finkel article in *National Geographic*, December 2007
http://www.mamamedia.com
http://www.mendonline.org/articles.html 'Nonviolence: The Only Rational Choice'
http://www.openbethlehem.org
http://www.palestine-family.net
http://www.palestine-family.net/index.php?nav=6-19
http://www.ploughbooks.co.uk
http://www.tikkun.org
http://www.un.org/unrwa/access/BedouinReport_May06.pdf
http://www.wfp.org – World Food Programme
http://www.youtube.com/watch?v=OqUNyEcUGnQ

Media

Stourton, Edward, *A River Runs through It*, documentary programme on the River Jordan, September 2009, BBC Radio 4.

Index